CALIFORNIA

Designing Freedom

Justin McGuirk and
Brendan McGetrick

FOREWORD

DEYAN SUDJIC

California is a place that the rest of the world keeps coming back to look at, and to learn from.

For Reyner Banham, the English architectural historian, Los Angeles was, as he put it in the 1960s, the place that persuaded him to 'learn to drive so that he could read it in the original'. The result was his remarkable book, *Los Angeles, The Architecture of Four Ecologies*, still in print almost fifty years later, in which with wit – and striking originality – he set out to upturn the conventional idea of the city as a brutally ugly anonymous wasteland of kitsch fast-food outlets and freeways. Los Angeles certainly did not look like the conventional idea of a city, but it offered a potent vision of what a different kind of urban life might be like, one which has continued to seduce the world.

Banham's book, though it used the word architecture in its title, was not directly about architecture, but it offered a way of understanding this city that, to Europeans, seemed so unfamiliar.

The Design Museum's exhibition on California does the same for a new kind of California that has evolved rapidly since Banham started taking driving lessons. Banham identified a counterculture of surf and customization. What he did not foresee was the extent to which that counterculture would transform itself, and become dominant in California. The geek hippies of the Homebrew Computing Club have inherited the earth, and are now in control of some of the world's most valuable companies.

We are now in a period when California has become part of the world's aspirations. It has its drawbacks: an inability to balance its budget, for example; a reluctance by wealthy homeowners to play their part in supporting less affluent downtowns by paying property taxes; and punishingly long commutes that will likely become unsustainable without cheap petrol. But it is also the place to which people come to make their fortunes, or to learn and attempt to replicate the success of Silicon Valley in other parts of the world. When Mike Bloomberg was still mayor of New York, Stanford was the university that he tried to persuade to set up a campus on Roosevelt Island.

Banham was perceptive in his understanding of Los Angeles but he had a blind spot about Northern California, which he all but ignored. For him, Los Angeles was the special place because, he claimed, it had originally been settled by land. So the pioneers arrived there having soaked up and learned from all that America had to offer on their way across the continent. San Francisco, however, was an etiolated east-coast transplant that had been settled directly by sea. As it turned out, of course, San Francisco and its environs have, over the last two decades, done as much to change the course of design and the way that we all live today as any city, anywhere.

This book and the exhibition that accompanies it explore just what it is about California that has allowed it to do that, and what gives the very word its power.

SELLING FREEDOM

Tools of Personal Liberation

JUSTIN McGUIRK

The phrase 'California design' conjures up a casual mid-century modernism: a poolside lifestyle furnished by Charles and Ray Eames, housed by Richard Neutra and photographed by Julius Shulman. Seductive though that canon is, it has very little to do with the hold that California designers have on the world today. Eames furniture may have become a global default setting, but it is the digital tools emanating from Silicon Valley that dominate our attention. California Modern has been superseded by California Mode, a way of being in which the individual can express himself or herself to a hyper-connected world – one's thoughts, one's experiences, one's lunch. Californian tools put information at your fingertips but they also turn you into information. This is our new global reality, as true in Phnom Penh as it is in Palo Alto. To know this is to recognize that designers at Californian companies are shaping the nature of the twenty-first century.

This shift in what we mean by 'California design' – from post-war interiors to global communication tools – is the story of how design itself has evolved as a discipline. Furniture and domestic products have ceded their place in our lives to *devices*: things with screens, operated by software and experienced through user interfaces. These are the tools of the information age, and the design that makes them so powerful, so intuitive, so easy to use, so addictive – or not – is design for the information age. The fact that we now carry super-computers in our pockets and that we mediate the world through screens has spawned whole new categories of design: software design,

User Interface (UI) design, User Experience (UX) design, interaction design (the terms are often interchangeable). The designers who deploy these skills have an almost creepy influence on many of our most day-to-day activities – the way we work, the way we communicate, the way we play. And that fact makes California, the home of so many tech giants, the global centre of design innovation.

The San Francisco Bay Area is home to probably the densest concentration of designers in the world. They are there because Silicon Valley's technology industry needs them. Design is what makes technology useful and accessible to ordinary people. Without designers shaping the human experience of a product, no piece of tech would make it to market. It is no coincidence that the technology firm that took design most seriously became the most valuable company in the world. Apple's platonic product design and intuitive software suggest that design is the difference between mere success and global domination. Subsequently, 'Designed in California' has become a globally recognized standard, like 'Made in Italy'. This tagline – which Apple stamps on its products to present them as home-grown goods, despite their being made in China – has become so powerful that even competitors on the other side of the world use it. Samsung is only one of many foreign technology and automotive companies to open design studios in California, all hoping that some of the native design culture will rub off on them.

However, this book and the exhibition that it accompanies are not just about design for technology. They take California design as a more

Above: Advertisement for the Apple iPad, 2013
Page 8: A Polaris A1 missile fired as part of the first submerged missile launch, Cape Canaveral, 1960

expansive idea. The guiding principle is that California has specialized in creating *tools of personal liberation*. Each of those words requires some defining. What do we mean by tools? And what is personally liberating about them? The answers lie somewhere in the mythos of California itself.

As the edge of a continent, California has always been a frontier. Since the nineteenth century it has been a place calling out to those in search of new opportunities, those who wanted to reinvent themselves. It is a place defined by successive booms: the Gold Rush, oil, military manufacturing, the dot-com bubble and whatever history will call the current boom in tech culture. Each boom has required fresh blood and new tools. Like the Netherlands, whose design culture is rooted in its having reclaimed the very land from the sea, California is a place that has made cities out of deserts. It spends forty per cent of its electricity simply moving water around, feeding those verdant lawns under dry, blue skies. California is the *ur* state of what Jean Baudrillard proposed was Utopia Achieved: a place that 'allowed itself to imagine it could create an ideal world from nothing'.[1]

The tools associated with a place reveal the nature of the place itself. The British critic Reyner Banham made much of the 'gizmos' that were used to conquer and civilize the West. What starts with Colt and Winchester rifles and bags of nails ordered from the Sears, Roebuck & Co. Catalogue evolves into transistor radios, waste-disposal units and outboard motors – anything that liberated the individual to live the perfect suburban lifestyle. Today's gizmos are even more portable,

more versatile, more powerful. Our computers, smartphones and apps have conquered new frontiers, once dubbed the 'electronic frontier' or 'cyberspace', virtual worlds where we can create our own image of ourselves. And the nature of this new culture of mass individualism owes much to California in the 1960s.

The counterculture of the 1960s in many ways defined itself against the relative affluence of 1950s America – that same perfect, suburban lifestyle – because it was an affluence associated with bureaucratic jobs; subservience to the military-industrial complex; the politics of segregation; and, ultimately, the Vietnam War. This youthful rebellion manifested itself in two ways: one was overtly political and the other was essentially anti-political. Those too disillusioned with politics to protest often withdrew from mainstream society to start afresh in a primitive, rural idyll. Between 1965 and 1972, several thousand communes were founded in the United States, with tens of thousands of hippies and other young people choosing to return to the land. These New Communalists, as Fred Turner has called them, needed new tools.[2] Some of these were tools of consciousness, LSD being the drug of choice for those seeking to free their minds. But there were also the hand tools and other gizmos that they required to make themselves self-sufficient. And these could be found in the countercultural equivalent of the Sears and Roebuck 'bible', the *Whole Earth Catalog*.

Founded by Stewart Brand, the *Whole Earth Catalog*'s strapline was 'access to tools', and it collected together those essential to setting up

'1984' – the Orwell-inspired television advertisement for the Apple
Macintosh, directed by Ridley Scott, 1984

your own community. Most of these were books, suggesting that information was the ultimate tool of self-transformation. But there were also tools of a practical variety, ranging from shovels and sewing machines to Richard Buckminster Fuller's geodesic domes, which were easy to assemble and whose distributed, connective structure was the perfect emblem for the communes' ambitions to be non-hierarchical societies. The do-it-yourself culture promoted and facilitated by the *Whole Earth Catalog* was very much in the tradition of earlier frontiersmen, and in the spirit of American individualism. In theory, at least, the communalists were independent, self-sufficient and in control of their own destinies. As Brand put it, 'We are as gods and might as well get good at it.'

When the short-lived commune movement began to unravel in the 1970s, and the counterculture with it, Brand was adept enough to hitch its ideology to the hackers and computer engineers in the San Francisco Bay Area, who were at the forefront of a different kind of revolution: personal computing. Still a tool of the military and the corporation, the computer was in the process of being made accessible to the individual. And that meant putting a device of enormous connective and processing power in the hands of rebellious world-makers – in this case, the geeks of the Homebrew Computer Club, which included the likes of Steve Jobs and Steve Wozniak, the founders of Apple. For Brand, this was another project in which tools developed by 'the system' – the defence industry and the corporations – could be hacked to create new communities and to liberate the individual.

This shift from the tools of the counterculture to the tools of the 'electronic frontier' has been well documented by Turner and others. In essence, the argument is that the new tools of personal liberation are our personal communication devices. And the implications for design culture are enormous. If mid-century modernism put California on the design map, that was largely a Southern Californian phenomenon – whereas, with the personal-computing revolution, the influence shifts to the Bay Area, with Silicon Valley as its epicentre.

The new design culture that flourished around Silicon Valley was the product of highly specific conditions, and its origins lay in the military. In the 1960s, the valley's largest employer was the aerospace company Lockheed Missile and Space, and until 1972 most silicon chips were used in Polaris missiles. But the culture of Silicon Valley is actually the result of a network of military, corporate and academic institutions. One of these was Xerox PARC, the research company that pioneered so many advances in personal computing, including the graphical user interface that made desktop computing possible. Another was Stanford University, which remains enmeshed in the corporate and research culture of the Bay Area. The proximity of these institutions, and the vast reservoirs of venture capital on offer, created a magnet for those with computer-engineering and design skills. As Barry Katz points out[3], the frenzied start-up culture that ensued had something of the quality of the city of Manchester during the Industrial Revolution – where trades, suppliers and entrepreneurs fed off each other symbiotically –

Material Design, the design language developed for Google's mobile interface, 2014

and correspondingly has made Silicon Valley the economic powerhouse of the US.

One might argue that California's magnetic pull on designers is as much sociological as it is technological or economic. If you speak to someone from Apple or Tesla, they will tell you that their companies could not have sprung up anywhere else. That is in part due to the state's nexus of technology and finance, but it is also because of an attitude. The nature of Californian exceptionalism is rooted in an ethos that is entrepreneurial and individualistic. It fetishizes risk and speed – 'move fast and break things' as Facebook has it – to play a zero-sum game of enormous stakes. But this ideology also stems from a deep-seated belief in putting tools in people's hands. These might be 3D printers, search engines, smartphones, apps, fitness trackers or batteries for storing solar power. Tools are what enable the individual to aspire to self-sufficiency, even if that is an illusion. They promise independence, be it from government or a nine-to-five job. Freedom is, to use the marketing jargon, California's unique selling point. And selling freedom is what California design is all about.

California's supreme tool is the screen. The Golden State has given birth to two great screen cultures: one is Hollywood and what we wistfully call the silver screen, and the other is the pixelated portal of the computer. The former is a Southern Californian phenomenon and the latter is decidedly Northern. While the crux of this argument relies on a Bay Area vision, Hollywood and other Southern Californian institutions have helped colour that vision. Herb Ryman's design of Disneyland, for

instance, was a perfect analogy for the state itself: it included zones called Frontierland, Tomorrowland and Fantasyland. California's unique ability to manufacture fantasies is borne out in the film industry, naturally, but also in tech culture. Hollywood has been the tech industry's perfect counterpart. Films like *Minority Report* reveal a feedback loop between the two, whereby Hollywood visualizes nascent innovations such as augmented reality in ways that become self-fulfilling prophecies.

It is through Hollywood that those who have never been to California feel that they know the place, but it is through that other screen culture that we enact daily the California Mode. We mediate the world through screens. Our smartphone may well be the first thing we touch in the morning and the last thing we put down at night. It is our portal to our social networks, our entertainment systems, often our work. And banal though this may be to point out, every one of those experiences is shaped by a designer. The proliferation of digital devices has prioritized design for the information age. As Stewart Brand famously pronounced, 'Information wants to be free.' In other words, it wants to be democratized, placed in people's hands like any other tool – except that it is the most empowering tool of all.

The personal computer is what made access to information so easy, and it gave rise to a design culture very different from the one that was defined in Europe in the early twentieth century. Personal computers, and the profusion of digital tools that followed them, only became ubiquitous thanks to

a whole new category of design: UI design. This nascent discipline came into being at Xerox PARC with the advent of desktop computers. Xerox's Alto and its successor, Star, introduced the graphical user interface as a way for those who were not familiar with code to use computers. Apple's 1984 Macintosh, though, was the breakthrough that really set the computer on course to becoming a household object. Developing on Xerox's innovation of the graphical user interface, Apple introduced the system of windows, folders, drop-down menus and a set of icons by Susan Kare – a cursor, a trashcan – that remain mainstays of computing to this day. It was not just the portable size of the Macintosh but its UI design that enabled Apple to frame this product, in a Ridley Scott-directed TV ad, as a victory for the individual hero over a faceless, Orwellian authority – as a tool, in other words, of personal liberation.

The very idea of the 'interface' has implications for design that go far beyond computers. This new discipline, which brought graphic designers and programmers together, put the designer in an increasingly strategic position. As it was professionalized, the role of the designer fundamentally changed. For one thing, the idea that the designer's job is to create a seductive skin around an engineer's machinery (as Raymond Loewy did) is patently no longer the case. The design of the interface determines both what the engineer needs to deliver and how the user will behave. Indeed, with digital tools, in which the functionality is provided by something as small as a microchip, the modernist certainties of 'form follows function' become debatable.

One might even argue that it is through California's pioneering of design for digital-communication tools that the very field of design exploded out of its traditional boundaries. After all, California's other major contribution to the evolution of design is 'design thinking', a not uncontested discipline that proposes design as a methodology applicable to business, to healthcare or to social problems as much as to the design of, say, a mattress. What could be more liberating than a new way of thinking? It is no coincidence that IDEO, the consultancy that champions design thinking, was founded by the same pair, Bill Moggridge and David Kelley, who helped frame and professionalize interaction design (Moggridge's term for User Interface design) in the 1980s. One can be forgiven for asking – indeed, people seem to be constantly asking – where the edges of design lie. California has energetically blurred those edges. Silicon Valley companies are 'designing' artificial intelligence. IDEO 'designs' school systems. Airbnb aims to 'design' the perfect guest experience.

Silicon Valley may have changed design but it did not always recognize design's potential. It was Apple that secured the primacy of design as a business's intangible adder of value. It was also Apple that framed digital tools as explicitly liberating. Jobs' and Wozniak's launch of the Apple 1 established the origin myth of the hacker – the amateur, the hobbyist – as the conduit between the technocrats of the military-industrial complex and the individual. The Apple 1's handmade wooden case was a direct link to the hippie, maker culture of the communes. Later, of course, that hacker aesthetic was shed in favour of an Ulm-school minimalism that makes Apple products the apotheosis of *gute form*. What began with the snow-white language of the Geman product designer Hartmut Esslinger evolved into the candy colours, and then the Braun-type smoothness, of the British Jonathan Ive – two émigrés among many, including IDEO's Moggridge and Tim Brown, lured to California like previous migrants were by earlier booms.

Apple's position in the top ten of Fortune 500 companies owes much to a steady stream of revolutionary products, but also to a corporate structure that prioritized design. The Macintosh, the PowerBook, the iPod, the iPhone, the iPad – each of these tools ushered in some paradigm shift or other: the ability to work anywhere, to have a thousand songs in your pocket, to access literally millions of tools with the touch of a finger. But it was the ethos of total design that kept its competitors at arm's length. Apple's design culture spanned intuitive user interfaces, seductive product design and the moment the buyer consummated the relationship: the 'unboxing'. As one of Apple's lead creatives of the 1980s recalled, 'When Steve Jobs used the word "design", he was advocating everything from hardware, software, advertising, communication, and user experience.'[4] Apple and other tech giants are now complete design ecosystems, with large internal design teams. Things have changed since the days when Eliot Noyes at IBM or Ettore Sottsass at Olivetti kept independent studios – the value of design has been internalized.

Even Google, which spent a decade proudly ignoring design, has shifted gear. Now all its platforms, from Android to Search, share a common language: Material Design. The very name acknowledges that the computer code and graphic symbols that we tend to think of as immaterial are, in fact, a design material that can be shaped like plastic. Like Apple's iOS, it guarantees a consistent brand experience. In the age of the planetary-scale platform, with a digital service reaching billions of people in hundreds of countries, the streamlining of every interaction is paramount. For that reason, the graphic language of smartphone-operating systems has been universalized. The old skeuomorphic icons have been tightened up into a flat, prim neo-modernism: a new International Typographic Style.

This Northern universalism is a far cry from the Southern Californian sense of what liberation through design might look like. In the 1980s and 1990s Californian graphic design was best known for the grunge-style cut-ups and idiosyncrasies of the LA-based David Carson and the expressive fonts of *Emigre* magazine. LA's scene has always been less puritanical and more about the pursuit of pleasure. A tool of personal liberation in So Cal is just as likely to be a surfboard or a skateboard.

Though something of an over-simplification, one distinction between the Northern and Southern Californian design cultures might be this: the Bay Area makes the tools, and LA produces the individuals who push those tools to their fullest expressive potential. This is certainly true of April Greiman, one of the first designers to demonstrate the graphic capabilities of the Apple Mac. Similarly, Frank Gehry pioneered the use of CAD drawing (through a French aerospace variant called CATIA) to express himself more freely. In doing so, he arguably did more than any living architect to liberate architecture from the right angle. But he did it for his own art. The Northern sensibility, if one can call it that, is to create tools geared to mass individualism; the Southern one is to embrace personal expression, body and soul.

The power of Silicon Valley's tool-makers – Apple, Google, Facebook, Twitter and many others – stems from being 'platforms'. The very concept of the platform embodies one of the defining impulses of California, which is to empower the amateur. Desktop publishing brought the power of the printing press into the home, and Internet platforms have revolutionized the media through user-generated content. The democratization of tools is leading to new forms of distributed manufacturing and new models of networked living. The Maker culture, which began in California and has spread around the world, and Tesla's Powerwall solar-energy system both promise independence from traditional industrial systems. They suggest a new era of mass self-reliance and a decentralized society. Forget Marxian notions of workers' solidarity – as Fred Richardson, one of the editors of the *Whole Earth Catalog*, put it, 'workers of the world, disperse'.

California's faith in the liberating effects of technology has spawned a zealous rhetoric. The July 1997 cover of *Wired* magazine announced, 'We're facing twenty-five years of prosperity, freedom and a better environment for the whole world. You got a problem with that?' This swagger bespoke a belief not just in technology as a social and economic panacea but also in the free market. The spirit of the counterculture was recast as techno-utopian entrepreneurialism. The promise of the Internet conjured up new worlds of opportunity, an 'electronic frontier'. It was as if cyberspace were a new territory to be explored and exploited – recall that early browsers were called Navigator, Explorer and Safari. The Internet supercharged the Californian faith in the individual by connecting him or her not just to instant information but also to a global community. At its most idealistic, that meant access to the 'global mind' – open-source thinking, or crowdsourcing – but, at its most commercial, it meant a potentially limitless market.

One cannot celebrate the influence of California on design without acknowledging what, especially from a European perspective, is its dark side. Disruptive platforms, from Uber and Airbnb to Facebook, empower the individual at the expense of traditional forms of labour, media and society. At every turn, public institutions are undermined in favour of private ones – public transport is deemed irrelevant compared to the self-driving car, the relative reliability of journalism is waning compared to the mass dissemination of fake news on social media. The Californian ideology frames technology's liberation of the individual in libertarian terms. Richard Barbrook and Andy Cameron argued two decades ago that the West Coast ideologues 'want information technologies to be used to create a new "Jeffersonian democracy" where all individuals will be able to express themselves freely within cyberspace', the obvious flip side being that 'the technologies of freedom are turning into the machines of dominance'.[5] A useful tool for an individual multiplied by one billion becomes a radical monopoly, possibly a lever of control and certainly a risk of mass-surveillance.

But this is the interesting thing about the 'Californifying' of technology: the Californified individual is already surveilling herself willingly, without even getting to some Orwellian roving eye. To wear a biometric wristband that counts your steps is to surveil yourself. It may be because you want to stay healthy or achieve the body beautiful, but turning steps into data is supremely Californian – it is the Protestant work ethic on your wrist. Digital tools created by a self-improvement culture will be aimed at making you more productive, more healthy, more goal-oriented. Personal devices in this world view are not unnatural, they are what connect the body to a larger system – just like riding your mountain bike in the hills connects you to nature.

This fixation on the self goes far beyond our physical reality in 'meat space'. We now have a whole new realm online in which to construct our identities. If the communes allowed you to be a freer 'you' among others, to achieve the individual within the collective, that is also the promise of the Web. We can be ourselves and be part of communities of our choosing. We have endless platforms for self-expression, or just self-documentation. And every tweet and selfie feeds the system. The California Mode means turning yourself into user-generated content. That means that designers

at Apple, Facebook, Google and other tech companies have enormous influence on our behaviour – from the countless swipes and micro gestures that we use every day to the way in which we shape and project our identities. It also seems to be leading ineluctably to a condition in which we record ourselves in real time, all the time. Any worthwhile event must be recorded and shared, otherwise it may be doubted – 'pics or it didn't happen' was briefly a popular social media maxim. California has delivered the state that Guy Debord predicted in *The Society of the Spectacle* in which everything must be rendered as image.

We are vaguely aware that being ourselves or expressing ourselves through digital tools constitutes our commodification through data, but the utopian belief systems behind these products rub off on us somehow. We self-improve, we self-promote, we self-express, we treat ourselves like brands because *we* are the product. That is what makes us all Californians. California's emphasis on design for personal liberation is not about offering liberation *from* something but the liberation to *do* something or *be* something. It is about putting tools in your hands, so you can go where you want, say what you want, make what you want, see what you want and join who you want.

1 •   J Baudrillard, *America* (New York, 1988), 83.
2 •   F Turner, *From Counterculture to Cyberculture: Stewart Brand, the Whole Earth Network, and the Rise of Digital Utopianism* (Chicago, 2006).
3 •   BM Katz, *Make It New: A History of Silicon Valley Design* (Cambridge, Mass., 2015).
4 •   Clement Mok, quoted in *ibid.*, 71.
5 •   R Barbrook and A Cameron, 'The Californian Ideology', *Mute* magazine, vol. 1, no. 3 (1 September 1995).

GO WHERE YOU WANT

Tools of Movement and Escape

What better metaphor for California's concept of technologically-assisted freedom than the multi-level highway interchange, with its promise of ease of movement and high-speed connectivity (traffic willing). The development of laptops and other portable devices pursues a similar rhetoric, in which miniaturization and portability are explicitly marketed as liberating. The iPhone, with its ecosystem of apps and inbuilt GPS, accelerates the ability to do almost anything anywhere from a single device. Having Google in our pockets has made us infinitely more mobile. Now the traditional idea of the car as a tool of personal freedom is being supplanted by autonomous vehicles that drive so you don't have to. To go where you want is to help a machine learn.

THE GOOD PLACE, OR NO PLACE AT ALL

Silicon Valley and the Paradox of Place

BARRY M KATZ

Sir Thomas More, Lord High Punster of England, gave us the vocabulary in 1516, back in the day when wayfinding meant dead reckoning under starry skies and most people died within walking distance of where they were born: Utopia – the good (*eu*-topos) place, or the non-place (*ou*-topos), Nowhere Land, the place that is *so* good that it cannot exist except in the collective imagination. That about sums up the coordinates of Silicon Valley, the narrow strip of real estate that connects San Francisco and San Jose and that has, for sixty-five years, served as the technological incubator and economic 'engine' of California, the United States and the world. Tinted in equal measure by the earth tones of the counterculture and the pixelated screens of tech, Silicon Valley, like More's Utopia, is mired in paradox. Buyer of myths, beware: if it sounds too good to be true, maybe it isn't.

Several evenings each week I find myself sitting in traffic on Highway 101, flanked by the white luxury coaches that shuttle legions of dot.commuters back to their South-of-Market condos in San Francisco from the theme-park campuses of Apple, Google and Facebook (workers at the pre-Internet companies – Hewlett-Packard, Intel, Applied Materials, Lockheed – must drive their own cars). I am struck by the paradox that many of these people have spent the previous eight hours working on technologies that should make it unnecessary for them to sit in traffic – or, for that matter, to be here at all. When tweets can circle the planet at speeds unrelated to human experience; when distributed teams, virtual communities and social networks make it barely necessary to get out of bed in the morning; when meetings are held, classes are taught, surgical procedures performed and wars fought from ergonomic workstations, the clustering of people in time and in place captures the essential contradiction of the tools of personal liberation that are being created here. They include the Marin mountain bike that lets us escape to the solitude of Big Sur, and the GoPro action camera that uploads our adventure to YouTube; Patagonia gear that accompanies us into the wilderness of Yosemite, and the GPS-enabled iPhone that ensures that we'll find our way back; software from Google that lets us peer into our neighbours' homes from space, even as hardware from NASA lets us peer into space from our neighbours' homes. The experience of un-augmented reality, to paraphrase Walter Benjamin, has become an orchid in the land of technology.

From a strictly geographic point of view, 'Silicon Valley' refers to a featureless exurban landscape of mini-malls and mega-mansions bounded to the west by the scenic Highway 280 and to the east by the aging (and dreaded) Highway 101. In recent years, the gross materiality of wafers and disc drives has ceded pride of place to the invisible software engines that drive the new Internet economy, and 'the Valley' now encompasses the whole of the San Francisco Bay Area. It is a land of windsurfers and websurfers, of gated communities and homeless encampments, of congested post-industrial sprawl and uninhabited landscapes of primeval beauty.

Latitude and longitude are mere details, however, for Silicon Valley is defined not by geography but by networks. Just as star-struck hopefuls bring their dreams to Hollywood in the hope of hooking up, today's aspiring entrepreneurs are drawn to Northern California from China and India and Israel and France in the hope of LinkingIn – with the densely interconnected mesh of investors, coders, lawyers, inventors, hackers, engineers, professors and designers who populate the region in ever-growing numbers. James Dyson remarked to me during a visit some years ago that it is a bit like Manchester in the early heat of the Industrial Revolution: you needed a guy who knew how to bend copper tube so you walked up the street and found one – or give you some technical advice, or lend you some money or rent you a cheap space to work. The frontiersman's freedom to move across permeable boundaries, to explore uncharted territories without a fixed destination in mind, is the defining feature of the region that has, not coincidentally, given us Netscape Navigator and Google Earth.

Silicon Valley is, above all else, an ecosystem in the decidedly non-metaphorical sense of the term: a techno-ecological niche whose populations feed off one another in a symbiotic, mutually sustaining way. At the centre, to be sure, are the tech companies that have for sixty-five years been creating the tools with which the rest of the world will work, play and communicate: Hewlett-Packard and Intel in the 1970s, Instagram and Dropbox and LinkedIn today. These companies recruit the freshly minted PhDs, MBAs and MFAs of the local academic institutions, and return the favour by endowing the professors who teach them and the classrooms in which they are taught. A comple-mentary role has been played by the labs – the Stanford Research Institute, the fabled Xerox PARC, Atari Research Labs, Interval Research Corporation – which bequeathed to posterity the networked workstation, electronic gaming and the surgical robot. Law firms, starting with Wilson Sonsini in the 1970s, draft the charters of the Valley's start-ups and protect their intellectual property. The venture capital industry, whose investments in Silicon Valley dwarf those of the rest of the country combined, exists in a web of reciprocity with the research, engineering, legal and academic com-munities (the author first heard the term 'venture capital' in the lobby of the Stanford Faculty Club). They are all touched by the corporate-design offices, independent consultancies and boutique studios that populate the region with what is probably the greatest concentration of design professionals in the world.

It is also, like *Freud's Rome*, a palimpsest whose superimposed layers of ruins, restorations and revivals expose the vicissitudes of its history and of the peculiar forms of mobility that prevail here. Consider Facebook, which began as a dating site in the undergraduate dorms of Harvard but soon joined generations of prospectors who had headed west with the dream of mining California's gold. Upon arrival, the scrappy start-up settled into an upstairs suite above a bead shop in downtown Palo Alto. A few months after the iconic 'Like' button was launched, Facebook exploded out of its cramped quarters and moved across town into a mid-century manufacturing building in the Stanford Industrial Park, recently abandoned by Hewlett-Packard – more than a symbolic displacement as the age of test-and-measure instrumentation was yielding to the inexorable rise of life on the Web. 'Shipping product' at HP meant loading crates of signal generators, frequency counters, voltmeters and oscilloscopes on to trucks parked at a loading dock in the back of the building, but for Facebook it means firing a stream of electrons out into the cloud for beta-testing. As Facebook grew – it is now, to all intents and purposes, the third largest country in the world after China and India – even this proved inadequate, and the company moved into a fifty-seven acre Bayfront campus built in the mid-1990s for the then-flourishing Sun Microsystems.

Just as Freud was able to discern, in a single gaze, the Rome of the Etruscans, the imperial Caesars and the Renaissance popes, it is possible to see the age of hardware manufacturing, the building of a digital infrastructure and the triumph of social media in the crosstown migrations of Facebook. Never in world history has there been such a rapid succession of core technology platforms, and never in such a concentrated place. One can track the course of personal com-puting from its inception in Douglas Engelbart's Augmentation Research Center to the research prototype built at the Xerox Corporation's Palo Alto Research Center to its pristine resting place on the tables of the flagship Apple store in the radius of an easy bicycle ride.

As part of a recent project, appropriately dubbed 'Voyage of Discovery', I had the opportu-nity to reconstruct the formation of Silicon Valley from the driver's seat of a Volkswagen e-Golf tricked out by an engineering team at the Center for Automotive Research at Stanford (yes, 'CARS') with sensors, data recorders, video-input equip-ment and a roof-mounted 360-degree camera. We drove first to the garage, in Palo Alto's leafy Professorville, where in 1939 Bill Hewlett and Dave Packard assembled the audio oscilloscope that would launch the region's electronics industry; then on to the suburban garage in Cupertino where Steve Jobs and Steve Wozniak cobbled together 'the computer for the rest of us'; then past the

Above: Prototypes of Waymo's self-driving car, 2016
Page 18: Aerial view of Silicon Valley, 2013

attendant-less parking garage where Google stores its fleet of driverless cars. We made it back to the 'clean' garage at CARS in less than an hour, including stopping at a local drive-in for lunch.

Indeed, the lore of the garage is pervasive in Silicon Valley ('Design Garage' is the name of the year-long entrepreneurial design sequence at the Stanford d.school that begins with an extended need-finding exercise in the autumn and ends with a product launch in the spring). What it symbolizes is the impatient culture of the start-up, its disdain for the sterile landscape of generic tilt-ups and beige cubicles. The iconic office building of the rapidly receding, pre-digital age is surely San Francisco's Transamerica Pyramid, whose steeply tapering form mirrors the organizational chart of the modern corporation: C-suites at the apex, crowning descending tiers of senior vice-presidents, aspiring executives, white-collar office workers and (out of sight in the proletarian basement) the custodial staff. Not so with life in the family garage, the converted storefront or the Mountain View café that doubles as an incubator, accelerator and co-working space. These ad hoc structures are dedicated to the proposition that we're all in this together, on an equal footing, writing the rules as we go along and ready to pivot on a dime: the engineer will do a bit of bookkeeping, the UX researcher knows how to code, the CEO runs errands, the designer does not wait to be handed a box full of components but is involved in the process from beginning to end.

Thirty years ago, the suggestion that the Bay Area might some day become a centre of design would have been met with bemused smiles from the ateliers of Milan, Paris, London, Tokyo or New York, but today – driven by the ideal of mobility and grounded in the relentless pursuit of miniaturization – this is incontestably the case. In 1972 Hewlett-Packard gave the world its first glimpse of the handheld in the form of the HP-35 calculator, a mobile device whose form was established by the design team before the engineers had even begun their work. By the end of the decade, a cadre of 'technopreneurs' – Adam Osborne, British expatriates John Ellenby and Bill Moggridge – had managed to shrink the computer to the dimensions of a suitcase (the 'luggable' Osborne 1) or a briefcase (the GRiD Compass). Guided as much by design as engineering, the computer had begun its journey from the desktop to the laptop to the palmtops of an ever-expanding user group.

The integration of design into the operations of the edgiest Bay Area companies is evident at Uber, where 180 user-experience designers work elbow-to-elbow with the engineering staff to ensure that passengers get where they want to go, when they want to get there and in the manner in which they want to travel. It is on display around the corner at Airbnb, where designers, engineers and researchers huddle together in conference rooms decked out in the spirit of the firm's most disruptive destinations. And at Amazon's Lab 126 (1 = A, 26 = Z), designers are likewise involved in every aspect of the Kindle e-reader and the Fire tablet, from the navigation aids on their screens to the biodegradable inks on the recyclable cardboard boxes in which they are shipped.

Interior of Tesla's fully electric luxury vehicle, the Model S, 2016

The ascendancy of design in the Silicon Valley ecosystem is perhaps most striking at Tesla Motors, whose operations are triangulated between a headquarters in Palo Alto, a reclaimed GM manufacturing plant across the Bay in Fremont, and a design studio around the corner from SpaceX in Southern California. Franz von Holzhausen, who leads the design team at Tesla, also serves as the company's Chief Product Officer, effectively putting him in a position of authority comparable to that of Sir (or is it Siri?) Jonathan Ive at Apple. I asked von Holzhausen how his role at Tesla differs from that of the designer in more traditional sectors of the auto industry (he previously worked in the design studios of Volkswagen, Pontiac and Mazda). His answer was revealing: whereas design typically serves as a link in a chain stretching from R&D to marketing, at Tesla it functions more like the hub of a wheel, integrating all of its parts. Every square inch of the surface of the Model S is a function of mechanical and aeronautical engineering, transmission and battery pack, the interactive seventeen-inch panel on the centre console, and the underlying business model.

Although Tesla is the only major company to be building actual production vehicles here, the automobile industry – whose historic mission has been to give citizens the freedom to go where they want without dependence upon rail lines or bus schedules – is the latest to arrive in Silicon Valley. In the last ten years, nearly every major auto company in the world has established a research lab or innovation centre in the region: BMW, Volkswagen and Mercedes; Fiat, Volvo and Renault; Toyota,

Honda and Nissan; GM, Ford and Chrysler have all created listening posts staffed by a combination of industry expats and Bay Area locals who are engaged in primary research, technology scouting, recruiting and software development. The same is true for a network of secondary suppliers such as Bosch and Delphi; insurance giants, including State Farm and Allstate; and, inevitably, a plethora of Internet start-ups and upstarts whose apps help us to drive our cars, park our cars, find our cars, share our cars, service our cars, and buy and sell our cars.

The next chapter in the history of mobility, it seems, will not be written in Detroit or in Stuttgart or in Hiroshima, but in Silicon Valley, as it becomes increasingly clear that the automobile is essentially a data processing device on wheels and the 'information superhighway' is not just a catchy metaphor. Automotive.com, to take but one example, offers a plug-in adaptor that mines the vehicle's on-board data recorders while linking the connected car to the owner's connected home and connected office. Interactive software developed in Silicon Valley tells drivers of the hybrid Ford Fusion about the performance not just of their car's engine but of themselves. And with the formation of Waymo, Google's self-driving car project, the brave new world of automobility is passing from science fiction to working prototype.

Driverless cars already populate the neighbourhoods around the Googleplex, promising us the freedom not just to go where we want but to do whatever we want along the way: read, sleep, network and negotiate. Beginning in 2009 with a retrofitted Toyota Prius, Google went on to develop its own prototype – friendly and marshmallow-shaped so as not to frighten fellow motorists, who still expect to see a human being at the controls and such quaint peripherals as steering wheels and brake pedals. In lieu of a flawed, human operator, Google's driverless car sports a roof-mounted LIDAR system – essentially, optical radar – that generates a continuous 3D map of its surrounding environment and combines these dynamic data sets with preprogrammed precision maps of its location. Automobile manufacturers are scrambling to keep up, but the competition may come not from within the auto industry but from Apple, which will neither confirm nor deny the existence of its 'Project Titan' but has reported to the National Highway and Transportation Safety Administration that it is 'investing heavily in machine learning and autonomous systems'.

As development of the driverless car races forward, mass transit, in this epicentre of the new technologies of mobility, remains stalled; as Reyner Banham commented in his loving hymn to Los Angeles, anyone hoping to cross town via public transportation had better be prepared to stay overnight, and the same is true of the San Francisco Bay Area 500 kilometres (300 miles) to the north. It would appear that people are more likely to insist upon their freedom to sit in traffic than to brave the uncertainties of the region's trains and trolleys and buses. Only a few initiatives have sought to upend this ingrained culture of vehicular individualism.

Working out of the NASA Ames Research Center in Mountain View, skyTran is developing a high-speed, low-cost, energy-efficient Personal Transportation System consisting of an elevated MagLev track along which computer-controlled, two-passenger pods might someday race up and down the Peninsula. More ambitious is Elon Musk's proposed Hyperloop, which promises to fire commuters through a sealed vacuum tube from Los Angeles to San Francisco at an average speed of around 1,000 kilometres (600 miles) per hour – a journey that will last about thirty-five minutes. Hyperloop was conceptualized by his engineering teams at Tesla Motors and SpaceX, but, as he has done at Tesla, Musk has released his patents and at least three companies are now actively building components of the possible system on the basis of Hyperloop technology. And since (in contrast to neighbouring Las Vegas) what happens in California rarely stays in California, feasibility studies are underway for other routes, including Paris–Amsterdam, Cracow–Gdansk and Toronto–Montreal, as well as Dubai, China and Mars.

Projects such as these bring us close to the heart of the California dream of frictionless movement, seamless interfaces and the fusion and confusion of hardware and software, money and policy, technology and design. In the dreamworld of Hollywood we might encounter cinematic visions of possible futures, but in Silicon Valley the codes are being written, the companies formed and the investments made which will almost certainly bring these visions to life. It is not far-fetched to imagine a passenger emerging from her sealed Hyperloop compartment at San Francisco's soon-to-be completed Transbay transportation hub, hailing a driverless Uber from her iPhone 12, donning a next-generation Oculus Rift headset and, from the back seat, conducting a virtual business meeting with partners across town or across the ocean. Pretty much everyone in the tech community acknowledges that scenarios such as these will be commonplace within a decade.

Which brings us back to Thomas More, writing 500 years ago almost to the day: utopia, he warned, is merely the shining face of dystopia. Everything in human history tells us that there is a dark side to the wonders of technology – that, as the French urbanist Paul Virilio reminds us, the history of the locomotive is also the history of train wrecks. The ethos of exploration, the tools of navigation and the technologies of miniaturization and portability have given us greater freedom of movement than any previous generation could imagine, but we will also have to endure the negative impacts of hypermobility: rootlessness, transience, the erosion of physical communities and the steady displacement of direct human contact. As a species, we have been very good at anticipating the consequences of failure but not so good at preparing for the consequences of success.

Advertisement for the HP-35 calculator, 1972

Ubiquitous computing begins with a calculator. The HP-35, the first pocket digital device, set in motion a process of miniaturization that is still underway.

It is driven not by Moore's law but by Hewlett-Packard making a design decision – to make the calculator fit in a pocket – and the engineers fulfilling that design. It is so successful that soon after its launch HP is selling 1,000 a day.

The HP-35 marks the moment when design, as much as engineering, starts to determine a piece of consumer electronics.

The HP-65, a successor to the HP-35 and the first programmable pocket calculator, 1974

Promotional photograph for the HP-35, the first scientific pocket calculator, 1972

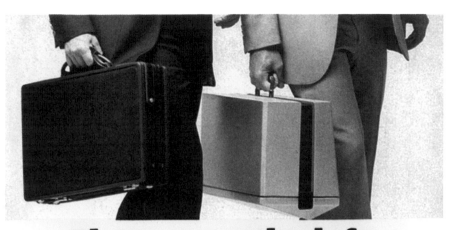

The guy on the left doesn't stand a chance.

The guy on the left has two file folders, a news magazine, and a sandwich.

The guy on the right has the OSBORNE 1®, a fully functional computer system in a portable package the size of a briefcase. Also in the case are the equivalent of over 1600 typed pages, stored on floppy diskettes.

The owner of the OSBORNE 1 is going to get more work done—and *better* work done—in less time, and with less effort.

Unfold it, plug it in, and go to work like you've never worked before. . . .

Go to work with WORDSTAR® word processing, so your correspondence, reports, and memos take less time to produce, and say more of what you wanted to say. And with MAILMERGE®—the mailing system that turns out personalized mass mailings in the time you'd spend on a rough draft.

Go to work with SUPERCALC®, the electronic spreadsheet package that handles complex projections, financial planning, statistics, and "what if" questions instantly. For the more technically minded, SUPERCALC will process scientific data and calculate results.

Go to work with powerful BASIC language tools—the CBASIC-2® business BASIC, or the Microsoft BASIC interpreter.

That's standard equipment.

Options include about a thousand different software packages from a host of vendors designed to run on the CP/M® computer system.

Go to work at the office, at home, or in the field.

Or anywhere. Optional battery packs and telephone transmission couplers mean you need never work without the capabilities of the OSBORNE 1. That's good, because you won't want to work again without it.

All for $1795. It's inevitable.

The OSBORNE 1 is the productivity machine that's changing the way people work. Put simply, the machine delivers a significant productivity edge—day in and day out—to virtually anyone who deals with words or numbers. Or both.

Since the entire system is only $1795, it won't be too long before the guy on the left has an OSBORNE 1 of his own. The same probably goes for the person reading this ad. In fact, we think it's inevitable.

The OSBORNE 1 includes a Z80A®CPU, 64K bytes of RAM memory, two 100 kilobyte floppy disk drives, a business keyboard, built-in monitor, IEEE 488 and RS232 interfaces for printers and other things that get connected to computers, plus CP/M, CBASIC-2, Microsoft BASIC, WORDSTAR, and SUPERCALC. The system is available from computer retailers nationally.

$1795. It's inevitable.

OSBORNE COMPUTER CORPORATION

26500 Corporate Avenue   Hayward, California 94545
Phone (415) 887-8080   TWX (910) 383-2021

Circle 325 on inquiry card.

BYTE December 1981   **33**

Advertisement for the Osborne 1 computer, 1981

The Osborne 1 portable computer, 1981

GRiD Compass laptop computer, 1982

Astronaut John Creighton with a GRiD Compass aboard Space Shuttle *Discovery*, 1985

The Osborne Computing Corporation and GRiD – two now forgotten companies. Yet the Osborne 1 is the first portable computer and the GRiD Compass, designed by Bill Moggridge, is the first laptop. The 1 is popular with businessmen, the Compass is limited to paratroopers and astronauts.

Advertisement for the Macintosh PowerBook, 1992

Apple's Macintosh PowerBook 100, 1991

Apple's Powerbook, on the other hand, is for the masses. 'Anywhere you want. Anytime you want.' With such slogans, Apple spearheads a soft-core political reading of the laptop, presenting it as the embodiment of freedom.

'Personal digital assistants' such as Apple's Newton and the Palm V mark a shift from the lap to the hand. They also herald a world of more personal devices with touchscreens.

The Palm V Personal Digital Assistant, 1999

Advertisement for the Palm V, 2000

The Apple Newton MessagePad, 1993

The Apple iPod portable media player, 2001

Advertisement for the Apple iPod, 2003

1,000 songs in your pocket, 200 books in your bag –
this is the numerical argument for hard drives as
entertainment devices. The iPod click wheel is the
piece of design that transforms a simple hard drive
into a wildly popular commercial product.

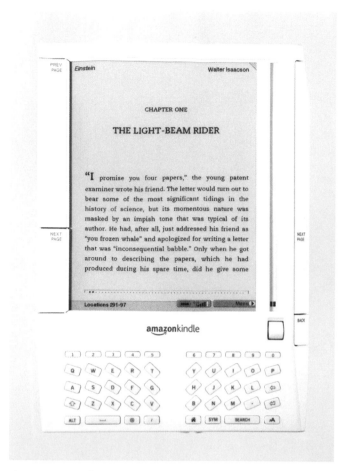

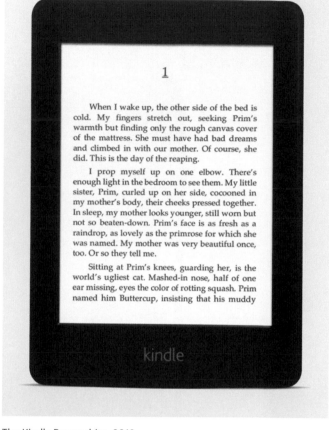

The Amazon Kindle e-reader, 2007

The Kindle Paperwhite, 2012

The iPod and the Kindle free us from CDs and books, and in the process usher in an immaterial world of downloadable 'content'.

Apple iPhone prototype, an antenna concept test model wrapped in copper tape, 2007

At its launch presentation, Steve Jobs describes the iPhone as 'Your Life in Your Pocket', 2007

The iPhone is a revolution in human behaviour.

Creating the archetype of the smartphone, the iPhone condenses a vast array of applications for communication, work and play into a pocket-sized glass oblong. As the applications increase, we spend more and more of our day looking at our phones.

None of this would have been possible without the invention of the 'Multi-Touch' touchscreen display. It introduces a world of apps – squares of digital real estate that open up into vistas of functionality. The phone operating system becomes a 'platform' for a potentially infinite number of tools, all accessible with a touch or swipe of your fingertip on the smooth aluminosilicate glass.

The Apple iPhone, 2007

Visualization of Google's mobile search, 2016

User interface design for smartphones gets ever more sophisticated. Google's mobile search interface responds to your location, suggesting local amenities and charting the most efficient path toward them.

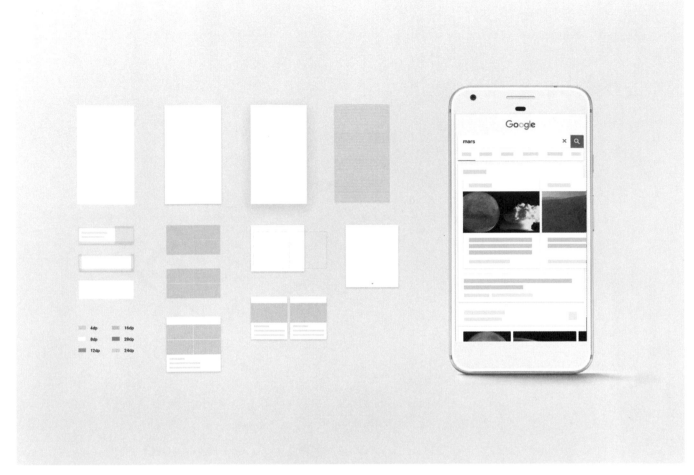

The components of Google's mobile search results page, 2017

The trick to making it intuitive and easy to use is establishing layers of information hierarchy. For a cohesive experience, all components are assigned specific line widths and heights. Behind the screen, there are careful specifications for every component and its placement on a page.

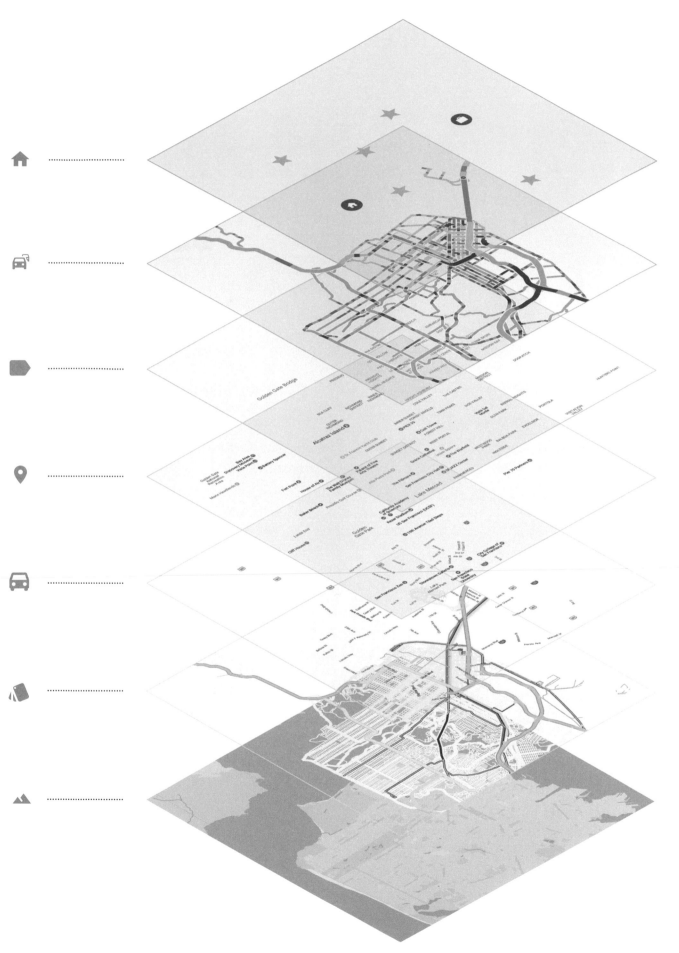

Your World
All the factual details of the map are framed around what's meaningful to you – places you saved, your upcoming events, custom home & work icons, even your own names for places.

Traffic
Traditional traffic light colours help you quickly interpret large amounts of information including data from local transport authorities and traffic incidents reported by people using Waze.

Neighbourhoods
Different sized areas are highlighted depending on how far you zoom and how dense the area is, helping you form a better spatial understanding of what you're looking at.

Landmarks
Highlighted buildings and natural features change as you zoom to help you orient yourself around recognizable points.

Road Labels
In densely populated areas, you'll see only the main road names, but zooming in reveals names for smaller roads to help you with more localized tasks.

Key Routes
Main roads & transit lines are highlighted with thicker strokes using adjustable stylesheets. Consistent colour palettes for parks, waterways and other features make the map glanceable.

Topography
The base map is a wireframe of vector shapes, continuously verified using satellite imagery to reflect new changes in the world.

Think about Google Maps as a piece of design. Traditional cartography is encoded with layers of data in a careful visual hierarchy. Major streets should be visible before minor ones, but zooming in takes you a layer deeper. These layers are flexible enough for up-to-the-minute traffic updates or the arrival of a new restaurant.

The Google Maps Pin, 2005

The map soon becomes three dimensional. Google's Street View camera takes 360-degree images that allow us to see accurate renditions of locations in the round. The Trekker is a personalized version mounted on a rucksack, for reaching inaccessible places. Google's camera has to be able to go everywhere so that we can see everywhere.

For the first time in human history, the map is now almost as big as the territory.

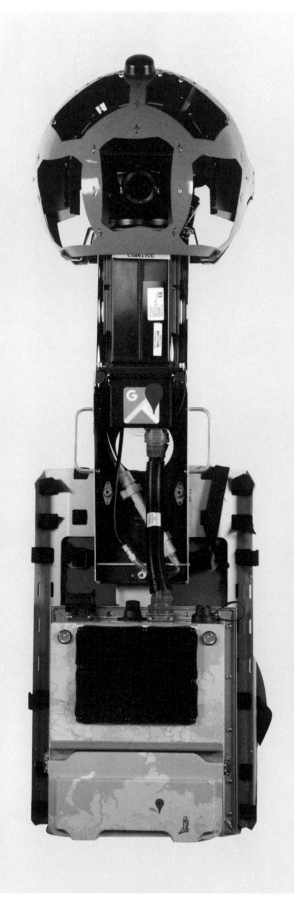

Above: Google's Street View Trekker Backpack fitted with 360-degree camera, 2013
Following Spread: The Google Trekker mounted on a vehicle in Samburu National Reserve, Kenya, 2015

Dennis Hopper and Peter Fonda ride through the desert in a scene from the film *Easy Rider*, 1969

In the 1960s, freedom is two wheels and an open road. In the 2020s, it will be not owning a car or even driving one, but putting yourself in the hands of artificial intelligence. The driver becomes a passenger.

Waymo's reference vehicle, Firefly, self-driving on the streets of Austin, Texas, 2015

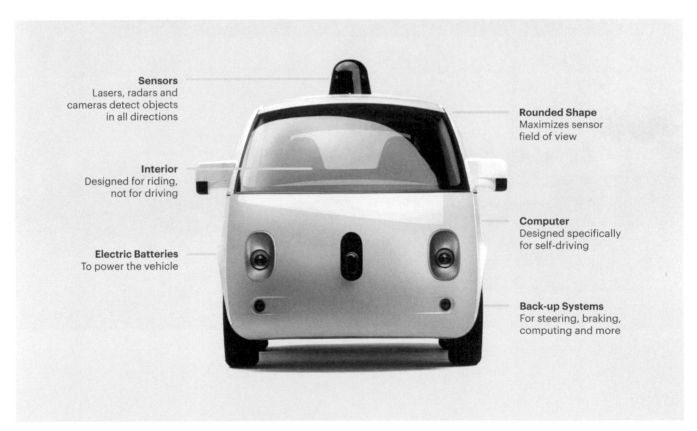

Sensors
Lasers, radars and cameras detect objects in all directions

Rounded Shape
Maximizes sensor field of view

Interior
Designed for riding, not for driving

Computer
Designed specifically for self-driving

Electric Batteries
To power the vehicle

Back-up Systems
For steering, braking, computing and more

Diagram of the key features of Waymo's self-driving car prototype, 2016

For a car to drive itself, it needs to know what's around it. Waymo's self-driving car can 'see' vehicles (pink), cyclists (red), pedestrians (yellow) and road works (orange) up to two football pitches away at any time.

3D representation of what Waymo's self-driving vehicles 'see' using sensors and software, c. 2012

The Fitbit Flex wearable activity tracker, 2013

'Get Moving', online advertisement for the Fitbit Alta, 2016

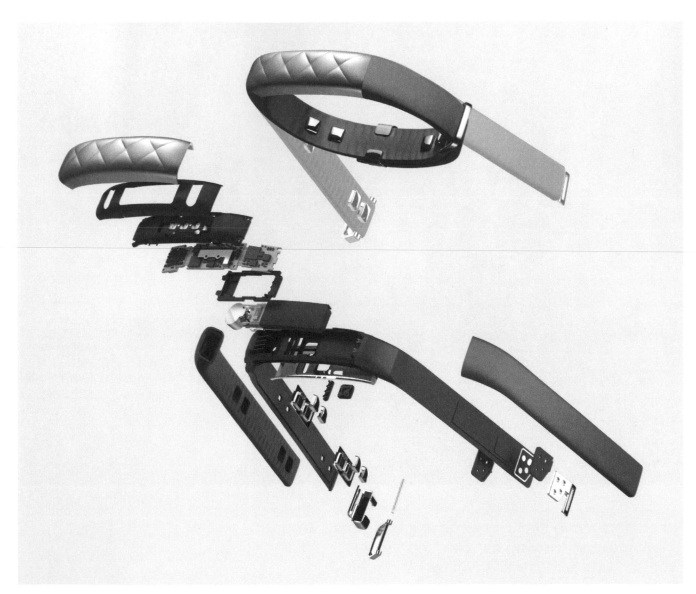

Components of the Jawbone UP3 activity tracker, 2014

TITANIUM F.R.S.
It doesn't get any better. Titanium 3 2.5 main frame. Fully suspended by Answer/Manitou front and rear. Touches of ano purple grace the matte dark gray titanium. Full Marin Lite componentry. This is one dream that could be yours.

25 lbs.

Weights listed are approximate to 1/2lb based on 17.5" bike w/o bar ends or bottle cages.

Advertisement for the Marin Titanium FRS Mountain Bike, 1993

Wearing biometric devices on our wrists is the Californian interpretation of the Protestant work ethic. Counting our steps is a form of self-surveillance that combines health obsession with a self-improvement culture. Walking must be productive and goal-oriented.

Biometric devices are the products of a data-driven culture. But California is also an outdoor culture. Mountain bikes and fleeces allow us to commune with the landscape and plug our bodies into the system that is nature.

Patagonia pile fleece cardigan, 1983

SEE WHAT YOU WANT

Tools of Perception and Fantasy

From Disneyland to Skywalker Ranch, California is a place that manufactures fantasy. This capacity for make-believe coexists alongside a commitment to inventing media and new ways of seeing the world. LSD, a tool of perception that helps shape the counterculture of the 1960s, offers a way to plug in to alternate realities. That tendency becomes mainstream with the development of video games, and is extended with tools that enhance our vision to create virtual and augmented realities. At the same time, the proliferation of tiny cameras has bred a culture that records and observes itself obsessively. To see what you want is to open doors to fantasy in the virtual world and self-surveillance in the real world.

STATE OF TRANSCENDENCE

Spiritual Technologies and the
California Dream

PETER LUNENFELD

California imagined itself into existence. From the very start, settlers had to be convinced to come here – by others, and by themselves. Northern California was in large part a product of the Gold Rush, which was itself created by people who convinced themselves that they would become rich mining for the precious metal. People did, of course, get rich – just not the miners. The people in San Francisco who became rich – *really* rich – were those who fed, clothed and lent money to the people who falsely believed that they were going to make a killing in mining. Ergo, the infrastructure of Northern California was built to service an endless flow of dream-chasers.

An entire industry was set up to lure people to the Golden State. Subsidies for the trip out West were paid for by real-estate interests, which, over the years, sold the travellers on dreams of a land where they could will themselves into Jeffersonian small stakeholders, real-estate sharpies, movie stars and moguls – or, if their compass pointed north and west, the grooviest of hippies or the techiest of billionaires. These are just a few of the dreams that keep people coming to California.

Perhaps the greatest dream that California sells is the idea that, in its forever sun-kissed embrace, you can do what you love. You can follow your passion; reinvent the status quo; make a real 'dent in the universe', in Steve Jobs's famous phrase. It is a fantasy tinged with truth, because when you come to California and achieve what you want it feels absolutely magical – like you've bypassed that long line of fantastically talented people in front of you in New York or Paris or

London. For more than a century, people have been streaming into California to avoid that line, though of course they created lines of their own on the freeways that carved up the state, and lines that never end in the most popular of the state's *sui generis* industries named after places rather than products: Hollywood and Silicon Valley.

Even in California's most saturated and competitive industries – the venture-fuelled tech north of Santa Cruz, and the entertainment-industrial complex south of San Simeon – there remains the sense that you – yes, *you* – have a shot. You may not be as beautiful as Brad Pitt, but you are probably better looking than Will Ferrell. And even if you lack a sense of humour, the California construct of reality television suggests that all you have to be is authentically yourself – and if you can do that well enough, then you, too, can ascend to the heights of Kardashianism. If being around the camera doesn't interest you, move up north, where all you need is an idea and the right pitch and *voilà*: you can become 'post-economic', pulling off an IPO and walking away with a billion dollars. With the right venture-capital first-round funding, you are – or could be – the next Larry Ellison or Mark Zuckerberg. *You* are the *next*. That's the California Dream.

The downside is what happens when you don't get it. And from the very beginning, California's pop culture has provided a diagnosis and a treatment for the stresses of a culture which demands that you do what you love. The first great Los Angeles novel, *Day of the Locust*, was written by a failed screenwriter who came to California to reinvent himself. Nathanael West had gained

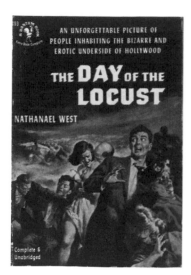

Above: Cover of the paperback edition of Nathanael West's
novel *The Day of the Locust*, 1953
Page 50: 'Orange Saturn', LSD-infused blotting paper, 1978

a bit of purchase in the entertainment industry, but never became a well-known screenwriter. His most famous book is about what it is to be amongst these people, who so desperately want to be a part of Hollywood but aren't. In the end, they burn the whole place down. San Francisco had already gone through its own, very real, fiery apocalypse after the great quake of 1906.

Geologically, and even climatologically, challenged as its setting is, the California Dream wouldn't have lasted this long without strategies for dealing with disappointment. This is another part of the fantasy, and Hollywood – and now Silicon Valley (the distinction vanishes as we stagger into the twenty-first century) – is central to this, too. In a society that insists that you live your dream, and surrounds you with others who make that look easy, how do you appease the majority who can't? California's answer is a blend of technologized pop culture and spiritual technologies. From the start, the entertainment-industrial complex has obsessively gauged, metricized and experimented with the intersection of desire and pleasure. It studies its audiences and develops genres that deliver exactly what they want, with just enough difference to keep them coming back. One of the masters of this approach was Walt Disney. Disney as a studio and Disneyland as a place were designed to be factories of desire, as opposed to factories of production. Disneyland set itself up as the reward for work. You work so that you can take your children to Disneyland. You're a good child, so that your parents will take you to Disneyland. You win the Super Bowl and Disney

pays the star player, when he's asked 'What are you going to do next?', to say 'I'm going to Disneyland!'

Disneyland, then, is the ultimate reward. It is a place in California that you must visit in order to experience the Wonderful World of Disney. At the same time, the Disney empire is ever-expanding beyond the place, absorbing the fantasies of the outside world into it. Whether the dream is to be a Beauty in love with a Beast, a toy come to life, a Jedi channelling the Force or a superhero enlisted to avenge, one company – based in the oft-mocked SoCal exurb of Burbank – has achieved hegemonic control over the fantasies that capture billions. Lest this be seen as a SoCal hegemony, however, do not forget that Pixar was the entertainment company founded by Ur-Silicon Valley-ite Steve Jobs, and that the moment director George Lucas made a pile of cash from his first space opera, he skedaddled up from Hollywood to acquire 2,000 hectares in Marin County to construct his Skywalker Ranch, whence he unleashed a never-ending stream of *Star Wars* sequels, prequels and collectible figurines.

Experiences in the worlds of Marvel, *Star Wars* and even Pixar ('To infinity … and beyond!' as Buzz Lightyear's catchphrase puts it) have the effect of priming a person for the technologies and lifestyles of the future. Apple, Google, Facebook, Twitter, Snapchat, Electronic Arts, Activision, Blizzard and so many more California dream factories surround these primed people in an augmented reality that is, in fact, the future now. The capacity to create the future and manifest it at this very instant is what makes California's particular ways of seeing so powerful.

Herb Ryman, Disneyland concept sketch, 1954

Over the last century, much of California's cultural production has been dedicated to preparing people for a moment that is coming. It shows ways of life that aren't yet familiar and suggests that they have already arrived in the Golden State – and if you've got any sense at all, you'll follow along. Whether you've ever even been to a beach with a surfable wave is immaterial; you'll dress like a surfer because, well, why wouldn't you want to snag some of that ineffable cool? Wearing a Bluetooth earpiece has always looked a bit silly, but doing so at one point – roughly ten years ago – made sure that people understood that you really grokked what it was to be hi-touch and hi-tech.

So many of California's new lifestyles revolve around new technologies of communication. The Doris Day/Rock Hudson vehicle *Pillow Talk* (1959) is a veritable cinematic treatise on telephonic connection in mid-century America (gently lampooned decades later by 2003's *Down With Love*). *Minority Report* (2002), for which Steven Spielberg assembled a group of future-technology experts including the virtual-reality developer Jaron Lanier, became the de facto model of how we expected to interact with computers in the future. In that future that is now our present, the physical components of the film-makers' vision come up short. However, the animation of the computer interfaces still offers inspiration to legions of engineers in Silicon Valley just itching for their own Skunkworks to develop Google Glasses, Snapchat Spectacles and whatever other mixed-reality products flow out of the Golden State.

In many ways, though, *Minority Report*'s influence is negligible in comparison with the defining California-specific science fiction film, *Blade Runner* (1982). Although over thirty years have passed since its release, the film's aesthetics have been impossible to escape. Visual designer Syd Mead's retro-deco architecture and scenic design, in particular, have become the look of an apparently inevitable future. We are just a couple of years away from 2019, when the narrative was set, and the build-up of downtown Los Angeles today, at a rate greater than any time in the past hundred years, is heavily affected by the combined imaginations of Mead; director Ridley Scott; fX specialist Douglas Trumbull; and, of course, the schizoid genius Philip K. Dick, on whose novel, *Do Androids Dream of Electric Sheep?*, the film was based. To this day, there have been very few science fiction films, or visions of any kind of futurity, that have been able to get past *Blade Runner*'s multilayered mix of technological futurism encrusted with accumulated grime and obscured by the haze of pollutants – a world of flying cars that you can barely see because of the smog, and impossible gadgets already looking worn with age.

The *Matrix* trilogy, the most celebrated sci-fi series since *Star Wars*, was for the most part the world of *Blade Runner* split into two halves. *The Matrix* (1999) remains a significant contribution to the visual imaginary of California, however, if for no other reason than that it introduced a binarism that will not go away in the twenty-first century. The film's narrative is driven by the choice between two pills offered to the film's hero, aptly

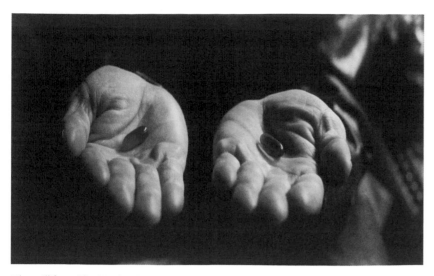

Film still from *The Matrix*, 1999

named Neo. The first will leave him unaware of the 'unreality' of the construct in which he has been living comfortably. The second reveals the 'real' real, a world of conflict in which he will be able to prove himself and save humanity from its machinic oppressors: 'You take the blue pill, the story ends. You wake up in your bed and believe whatever you want to believe. You take the red pill, you stay in Wonderland, and I show you how deep the rabbit hole goes.' The idea of a red pill that allows anyone to achieve the status of the Platonic philosopher escaping the cave of illusions is a powerful myth about the capacity of the entertainment/technology nexus to shift us into ever-newer realities.

This is particularly true in the online culture driven by Silicon Valley's lethal combination of physical devices that captivate and delivery systems that mutate, taking over our every waking moment, seducing with an unfinished and unfinishable aesthetic composed of sights, sounds and interactive interfaces. The belief in the power of technology to reveal the invisible has a long history in California. It starts with the region's rapid growth in the nineteenth century, when the state received a massive influx of people who had to build their own worlds. By the 1920s, there were more new religions being founded and followed in California than anywhere else on earth. In the 1950s, the science fiction author L Ron Hubbard created the epitome of these technology-tinged faiths with the Church of Scientology. By the 1960s, the human-potential movement (has there ever been a more Californian phrase?) was born in the Esalen Institute amidst the incomparable natural beauty of

Big Sur. The therapeutic technologies developed there from a meshing of psychology, Eastern metaphysical practices and a concentration on self-actualization were later synthesized by movements like Werner Erhard's EST (Erhard Seminars Training) seminars, and debased by many others – most spectacularly, the violent anti-drug cult Synanon.

Scientology, EST and even Synanon sprang from the peculiarly North American belief in 'spiritual technology'. LSD was viewed as a spiritual technology, a pharmaceutical route to the mystical realms of the divine – and boy, did it charm its way into the California Dream, especially up north! Victor Moscoso's psychedelic posters for rock concerts were aswirl with colour, and they both drove and were driven by the Bay Area Acid Tests – a series of parties held by author Ken Kesey – in the 1960s. In early experiments, computing and virtual reality were viewed in the same way – as technologies that could provide a glimpse into the beyond. The similarity isn't a coincidence: many of the fundamental innovations of computing were developed in partnership with LSD.

John Markoff's *What the Dormouse Said: How the Sixties Counter-Culture Shaped the Personal Computer Industry* (2005) maps the intersection of psychedelia and the digital. An essential character here is Douglas Engelbart, the visionary engineer who created the computational world in which we now live. His 1968 'mother of all demos' in San Francisco introduced live teleconferencing, scalable windows, text processing, collaborative real-time editing and an 'x-y position indicator for a display system' – the last-named far better

Game still from *World of Warcraft*, 2016

known as a 'mouse', because the cord coming out of the back reminded him of a tail. In other words, it was all there, ripe for the taking, way back in 1968. Later, Engelbart took his whole staff to the International Foundation for Advanced Study, where they dropped acid and strove to create the next new thing. Others followed them – including *Whole Earth Catalog* guru turned online community builder Stewart Brand, and Apple and Pixar founder Steve Jobs – championing psychedelics as key to the openness to develop new tools and systems for making 'a dent in the universe'.

These spiritual technologies are not without their terrors. There is a recurring fear that people will lose themselves in the tech, that they will give themselves over to parallel universes of fantasy that only they understand. These fears are not unfounded. Gaming, for instance, has evolved into alternative realities where power can be redistributed outside of inherited social constructs and hierarchies. The gamer can have mixed success at every other element in life, but within the gaming world – or within the still more specific world of a single game – he (and in these intensified situations, it's usually a he) can be respected, possibly admired. Similarly, in the world of social media, new status indicators are forming at the precise moment at which the social hierarchies linked to employment, which we inherited from the industrialized capitalism of the nineteenth and twentieth centuries, start to dissipate as jobs disappear. Products like the massively multiplayer online role-playing game World of Warcraft (published by Blizzard) and the photo-sharing application and

service Instagram (acquired by Facebook) offer their users new spaces in which to distinguish themselves. These spaces are emergent social spheres, meritocratic in their own ways, that provide, in the Californian tradition, methods for people to avoid the line separating their reality from their dreams.

No portal has been more important to California Dreaming in the past fifty years than that explored by transplant Aldous Huxley, an Englishman who relished Los Angeles' noonday sun. When he took a trip north to Esalen in the mid-1960s, Huxley famously lectured about passing through 'The Doors of Perception'. He called for the development of 'nonverbal humanities', and within half a century California-designed smartphones and California-organized social networks do not just encourage, but demand, that we communicate with icons and filters and images – emojis, thumbs-up 'Likes' and face swaps are nothing if not non-verbal. Part of the power of visual media, from television to gaming to online social spaces, is that they open new doors. By using them, we gain access to portals that have never before existed in human history. California has a large claim on the media and messages that augment our lives, delivered on screen, via electrons to the home, and on the street. The Dead Kennedys' punk anthem 'California Über Alles' isn't quite the right way to describe these phenomena, objects and systems. Better might be 'California Inter Alles', a state of technologized transcendence available anywhere, anytime, to anyone who buys into that which is designed in the Golden State.

'The Sorcerer's Apprentice', 1977

In the 1960s one tool of perception is prized above all others: LSD.

Made illegal in California in 1966, it continues to be distributed as tabs of acid blotting paper, with designs that signify its psychoactive properties. LSD is a tool of consciousness, opening the door to alternative realities – California's favourite place.

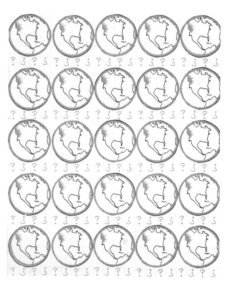

'California', 1985

'Surfing Shiva', undated

Victor Moscoso, 'The Chambers Brothers, The Matrix, San Francisco', 1967

Acid infuses the music and graphics of the counterculture. The psychedelic posters of Victor Moscoso, Rick Griffin and others are the official aesthetic of the 'Turn on, tune in, drop out' culture.

Victor Moscoso, 'The Doors, Miller Blues Band; Avalon Ballroom, April 14–15', 1967

Rick Griffin, 'Chuck Berry, Sons of Champlin; 1601 West Evans Street, Denver, November 17–18', 1967

Victor Moscoso, 'Big Brother and the Holding Company, Blue Cheer, The Charlatans; Avalon Ballroom, March 31–April 1', 1967

Allen Cohen, *The City of San Francisco Oracle*, vol. 1, no. 7, 1966

Paul Foster, 'Can You Pass the Acid Test?', 1965

Roger Webster, Environmental Communications, 1977

In the 1970s Los Angeles starts to be seen in a new light. The hopeless anti-city becomes valued for an authentic pop vernacular.

Environmental Communications, a group of architects and photographers based in Venice Beach, documents this landscape of billboards, gas stations, murals and hot dog stands.

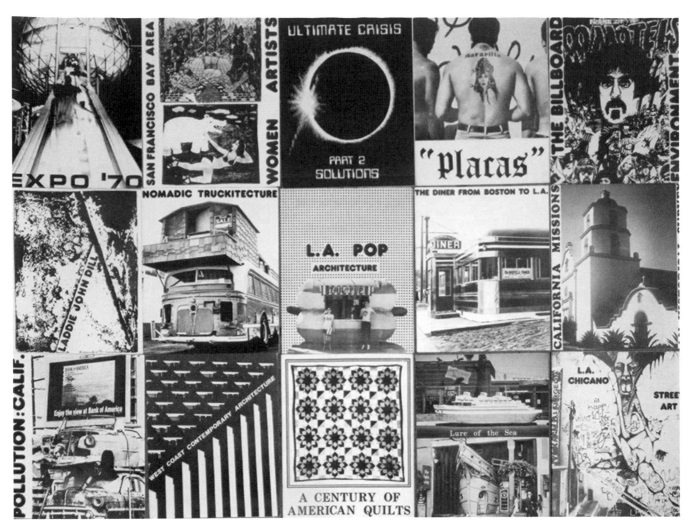

Publications by Environmental Communications, 1970s

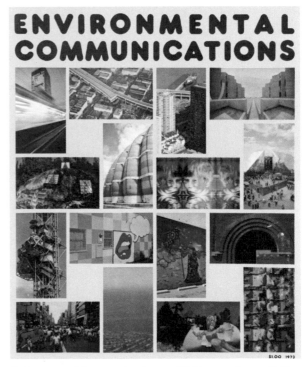

Environmental Communications, exhibition catalogue, 1973

Los Angeles Fine Arts Squad, 'Isle of California', 1977

Environmental Communications, hand-painted McDonalds billboard, 1977

Billboard from the opening title sequence of the BBC documentary
Reyner Banham Loves Los Angeles, designed by Deborah Sussman, 1972

The British architecture historian Reyner Banham
is enthralled by LA. His book *Los Angeles: The
Architecture of Four Ecologies* is a contrarian hymn
to the city's freeway culture, Googie architecture
and bungalow suburbs.

By the early 1980s, however, LA is enshrined in
a more dystopian vision by Ridley Scott's *Blade
Runner*. Visualized by the artist Syd Mead, the
film's scenography has become synonymous with
the future.

Above: Syd Mead, street scene
painting for *Blade Runner*, 1980
Following Spread: Syd Mead, concept
artwork for *Blade Runner*, 1980

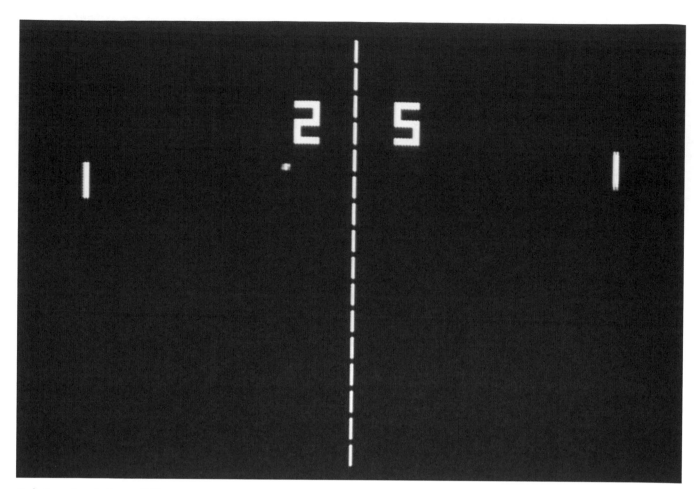

Atari, Pong Arcade Game, 1972

Video games open another door to alternative realities that leads ultimately to the creation of entire virtual worlds. It begins with a two-dimensional simulation of a table tennis game. Atari's Pong is a single pixel batted back and forth across the screen.

Promotional photograph for the Atari 2600 home video game console, undated

The Atari 2600 CX2600-A, 1980

The Google Cardboard low-cost virtual reality viewer, 2016

Now you can immerse yourself fully in virtual reality – to play, to design, even as therapy. If LSD was a 'spiritual technology' that enhanced perception, VR takes you deeper into the rabbit hole. It is media as total sensory experience.

Promotional photograph for the *Bravemind* virtual reality exposure therapy experience, 2005

Promotional photograph for the Oculus Rift virtual reality headset, 2016

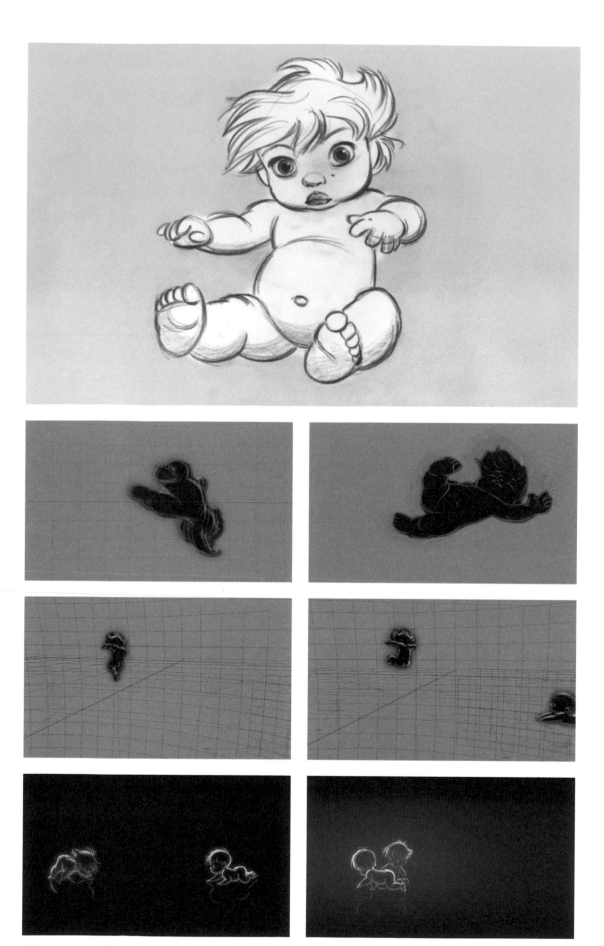

Stills from the making of *Duet*, an interactive film by Glen Keane, 2014

See What You Want

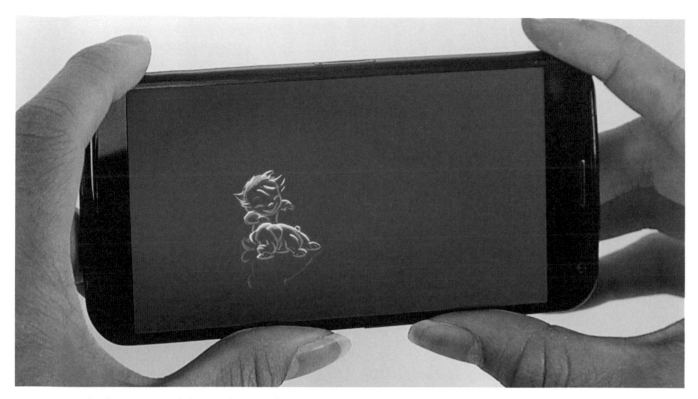

Duet, an example of interactive mobile-specific storytelling experiences developed by Google, 2014

Even Disney animators like Glen Keane are exploring how to turn hand-drawn animations into 360-degree worlds. In this spherical space, narratives are no longer linear but must accommodate simultaneous stories coming at you from any angle.

The Nest Cam indoor security camera, 2016

Still of video captured by Nest Cam and streamed to a smartphone, undated

The GoPro Hero 4 action camera, 2014

Video still captured by a GoPro camera, 2015

Our media tools have become tools of self-surveillance. We willingly – greedily – record ourselves. We turn our lives into data streams – not just for posterity's sake but because we increasingly communicate in moving images.

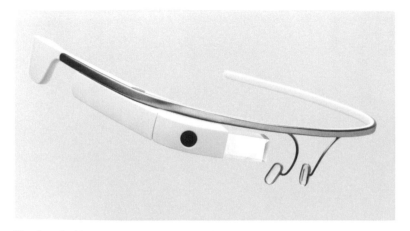

The Google Glass optical head-mounted display, 2013

Video still from 'Google Glass How-to: Getting Started', 2013

Above: Snapchat Spectacles smartglasses, 2016
Following spread: Promotional photograph for Snapchat Spectacles, 2016

Google Glass aims to embed perception with layers of data – the face computer.

Snapchat Spectacles turn that idea into a social media toy. Sunglasses that record what you see – a memory machine.

SAY WHAT YOU WANT

Tools of Self-Expression and Rebellion

The political agitation of the 1960s results in a surge of freedom of expression, from the Free Speech Movement at the University of California, Berkeley, to movements in support of civil rights for African Americans, women and the gay community. By the 1980s this activist graphic culture gives way to a new wave of graphic expression that is individualistic, anarchic and lifestyle-oriented. This anything-goes, Southern-Californian aesthetic is in stark contrast to the corporatized modernism of New York. Today, personal expression has been universalized – we can all broadcast our individualism but through the standardized interfaces of social media platforms. Now activists and presidents use the same formats to say what they want.

"ONLY ON THE BONES OF THE OPPRESSORS CAN THE PEOPLE'S FREEDOM BE FOUNDED-- ONLY THE BLOOD OF THE OPPRESSORS CAN FERTILIZE THE SOIL FOR THE PEOPLE'S SELF-RULE.

GRAPHIC DESIGN AS TOOL

Tools are Rules and Schools and other things

LOUISE SANDHAUS

An iconic 1976 *New Yorker* magazine cover by Saul Steinberg depicts a particular world view – that of the East Coast, and more specifically of New York, considering itself as the centre of the universe. The bustling terrain of the Big Apple dominates the foreground, while the United States west of the Hudson River is an uncertain yellow rectangle. One of the few distinguishing features of this distant landscape is a generic rock labelled 'Los Angeles'. California barely exists! Yet being a supposed nonentity can have advantages. Scarcely a blip on the radar, the Golden State was the place where people could escape the spotlight and resist 'the ways things were done'.

For graphic designers in the 1970s, at least from the New York point of view, the dominant 'way' wore the garb of seriousness – austere, rational and objective. Its attributes were machine-set, sans-serif typography rather than hand lettering; gridded compositions instead of random arrangements; photographic images as opposed to fanciful illustrations. These methods came from the Swiss, via early twentieth-century Constructivist typography. Swiss design, eventually called the International Typographic Style or high modernism, had the noble vision of a universal visual language of functionality and refinement, one that could serve and unite a global community recently divided by two world wars. Imported into the American context starting in the 1950s, however, Swiss design standards lost this political ambition and became, instead, a tool for corporate communication in the capitals of commerce – for the most part, New York and Chicago. They solved all design problems with,

essentially, grids and the use of Helvetica font – applying a similar, constrained look regardless of content. This uniformity was also easy to teach, and therefore became more fully entrenched as the 'right way' as it passed through generations of design students and instructors. Design became a monotone lacking distinguishing characteristics, accents or dialect. We were all speaking the design Esperanto of generic modernism.

And yet ... as the International Typographic Style commanded swathes of the East Coast and beyond, and everyone was playing along nicely, California was blazing a new trail.

Design innovation here was in full flow: fantastical motion graphics; ecstatic album-cover art; Supergraphics, which disrupted architectural space; and experimental schools redefining arts and design education. New ways of thinking were up for grabs, and visual form and media were being created seemingly from a different starting point.

Looking back, trying to identify the magic starting point that distinguished these designers at work, what may have been most radical were the tools they used. Not conventional design tools like pencils and T-squares – 'devices for doing work' – but rather manifestations of that other definition of tools, 'a means to an end'. This second idea opens wide territory. As a means to an end, a tool can be a set of rules, a school or even an abstract approach like an attitude or state of mind. In California these tools, as they were applied to graphic design, produced improbable outcomes. They liberated self-expression – personal and political – and provided a reconsideration of

Above: Saul Steinberg, cover of *The New Yorker* magazine, March 1976
Page 82: Emory Douglas, 'Untitled (On the Bones of the Oppressors)', 1969

process and purpose. If a tool can be a set of rules, can work be transformed from regulated rote to joyous experimentation? Can conversation be a tool? What if graphic design spoke *with* audiences, in their language, rather than *to* or *at* them? What might be said and, therefore, understood? How might society be transformed if graphic design was an instrument for dialogue, compassion and collaboration? Can graphic design transform consciousness? What if rather than looking *at* images, we journeyed *into* them?

In all sorts of ways California graphic designers – or those making graphic design (as they didn't all claim the moniker) – utilized new devices to reorient what they were doing. In the early 1960s Sister Corita Kent became head of her Los Angeles alma mater, Immaculate Heart College, running its art department under an ethos that she adopted from the Balinese: 'We have no art, we do everything the best we can.' Corita had developed a national reputation as a celebrated teacher, artist and designer, having booted capital-A 'art' off its pedestal and elevated, instead, the slogans and aesthetics of ordinary life into resonant works of graphic design. Initially, this vibrant agenda transformed spiritual messages and cultivated refreshing actions for people seeking daily sustenance; eventually, her output became oriented around issues including Vietnam and civil rights.

Yet one of her greatest legacies, just as radical though less widely known, is her manifesto for pedagogy, self-expression and studio practice – the 'Immaculate Heart College Art Department Rules'. As a tool, these rules reset the path for visual work,

abandoning judgmental binaries of good/bad and right/wrong and replacing them with a single target: simply 'make', joyously and copiously. Points of departure could include everything from readings to images and come from anywhere, from supermarket shelves to street corners. Discovery through looking, alongside stumbling through and manipulating any materials at hand, opened a pathway to imaginative outcomes that might marry the graphic circus of Wonder Bread packaging with a message on the wonder of God.

While Corita's Rules shaped a new ethos that was adopted for design ends, tools manifested by other graphic designers gave a one-two punch to political agendas. California was no stranger to inciting political momentum through the passion-provoked graphic vehicles of political posters, flyers and alternative newspapers, but designers Emory Douglas, Archie and Brad Boston, and Sheila de Bretteville cultivated tools that helped to further and reposition the conversation of positive social and political transformation.

Tools for Political Ends

Emory Douglas was a graphic designer who had first encountered the practice during a stint at a juvenile facility, and then studied commercial art at the City College of San Francisco. Inspired by Malcolm X's edict of 'self-respect, self-defense, self-determination', Douglas made social justice his cause, joining the Black Panthers as its Revolutionary Artist and Minister of Culture. From

IMMACULATE HEART COLLEGE ART DEPARTMENT RULES

Rule 1 FIND A PLACE YOU TRUST AND THEN TRY TRUSTING IT FOR A WHILE.

Rule 2 GENERAL DUTIES OF A STUDENT: PULL EVERYTHING OUT OF YOUR TEACHER. PULL EVERYTHING OUT OF YOUR FELLOW STUDENTS.

Rule 3 GENERAL DUTIES OF A TEACHER: PULL EVERYTHING OUT OF YOUR STUDENTS.

Rule 4 CONSIDER EVERYTHING AN EXPERIMENT.

Rule 5 BE SELF DISCIPLINED. THIS MEANS FINDING SOMEONE WISE OR SMART AND CHOOSING TO FOLLOW THEM. TO BE DISCIPLINED IS TO FOLLOW IN A GOOD WAY. TO BE SELF DISCIPLINED IS TO FOLLOW IN A BETTER WAY.

Rule 6 NOTHING IS A MISTAKE. THERE'S NO WIN AND NO FAIL. THERE'S ONLY MAKE.

Rule 7 The only rule is work. IF YOU WORK IT WILL LEAD TO SOMETHING. IT'S THE PEOPLE WHO DO ALL OF THE WORK ALL THE TIME WHO EVENTUALLY CATCH ON TO THINGS.

Rule 8 DON'T TRY TO CREATE AND ANALYSE AT THE SAME TIME. THEY'RE DIFFERENT PROCESSES.

Rule 9 BE HAPPY WHENEVER YOU CAN MANAGE IT. ENJOY YOURSELF. IT'S LIGHTER THAN YOU THINK.

Rule 10 "WE'RE BREAKING ALL OF THE RULES. EVEN OUR OWN RULES. AND HOW DO WE DO THAT? BY LEAVING PLENTY OF ROOM FOR X QUANTITIES." JOHN CAGE

HELPFUL HINTS: ALWAYS BE AROUND. COME OR GO TO EVERYTHING. ALWAYS GO TO CLASSES. READ ANYTHING YOU CAN GET YOUR HANDS ON. LOOK AT MOVIES CAREFULLY, OFTEN. SAVE EVERYTHING IT MIGHT COME IN HANDY LATER. THERE SHOULD BE NEW RULES NEXT WEEK.

Corita Kent, 'The Immaculate Heart College Art Department Rules', 1968

1967 until the end of the 1970s, he created posters and a weekly newspaper for the Black Panther Party. While the mainstream press depicted the organization as violent and militant, in the compassionate hands of Douglas the Panthers attained a more nuanced and three-dimensional public image, powerfully communicating sorrow as well as outrage. His designs forged a sense of community and a coherent political voice, spread awareness of government activities and rallied dissent over the lack of healthcare, education and food programmes. In his wisdom, out of habit or the convenience of the means at hand, Douglas deployed a visual vocabulary that resonated with the people, *his* people, because it was familiar. His designs spoke in the vernacular of a community.

At the time, had Douglas's work been seen at all outside his intended audience it would certainly have been dismissed as crude and naive by the self-righteous graphic-design establishment, which had little taste for political activism. Douglas produced messages laid bare, stripped of cleverness and self-consciousness. His drawing style sometimes favoured familiarity over refinement, resulting in simplistic renderings that could be immediately understood. He also produced bold collages and technically skilled portraits. His typographic elements, mostly rubdown lettering, were choices of convenience. Some posters presented daily lives of dreary, unacceptable conditions, against which a community could revolt, while others focused outrage towards police, civic leaders and US officials, depicting them as pigs, depraved in their treatment of the black community. In Douglas's deft hands, the vernacular became a powerful tool for social justice.

Attitude was another tool in the arsenal of design as a means to a political end. In the United States of 1965, regardless of region or city, commercial artists worked in advertising: it was the only game in town. The hierarchy resembled that of the TV show 'Mad Men', with bosses, creative chiefs and account managers in charge of everything, followed by copywriters and then the 'art guys'. Almost everyone was male and white. Women were anomalies. To be black was equally, or even more, unusual. And that brings us to the real-life story of Archie and Brad Boston.

After a few tough years in the LA ad biz, struggling to gain equal footing alongside white creative colleagues, Archie Boston joined with his brother and fellow graphic artist, Brad, to form the design studio Boston & Boston. Together, they confronted the status quo in an effort to join it. For starters, they used a typeface called Jim Crow for their logo. Instead of hiding behind an edifice of colour-blindness, the Bostons put their blackness out in front with a deliciously provocative sense of humour. Their attitude towards racism became a tool with which they built a business and reconfigured a problem into an asset. During 1966–7 they produced a series of self-promotions to exemplify the kind of work that they hoped to do for clients seeking a new level of audacity. One ad presents a Boston brother in Ku Klux Klan garb with the tagline, 'For a discriminating design organization ... call the BOSTON KLAN'. Another depicts shirtless Boston brothers draped in 'For Sale' signs. A third

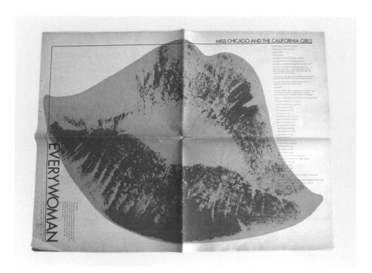

Sheila Levrant de Bretteville, *Everywoman* newspaper, 1970

promo, featuring an Uncle Sam pose, changes the famous 'I want you' recruitment slogan to 'Uncle Tom Wants You' (a reference to the devoted slave from Harriet Beecher Stowe's *Uncle Tom's Cabin*), in a witty and complex conflation of American historical icons – one of patriotism, the other of race betrayal.

This tactic of smart-ass attitude as a calling card was not received quietly by African Americans *or* white racists: the campaign drew plenty of offended comments. Unfazed, the Bostons knew that any reaction from this crowd mattered far less than a welcome reception from the Southern California audience that they hoped to reach. Said Archie Boston, 'We wanted to work with clients that were interested in working with designers that were daring and courageous enough to speak their mind.'

In 1969 Sheila de Bretteville, fresh from New York (and a year in Italy), arrived in Los Angeles to join the spanking new California Institute of the Arts (CalArts), then accepting its first students. De Bretteville began her role as in-house designer and faculty member in the School of Design in sync with her idealistic colleagues. Their shared motivation was to create a new model for pedagogy and practice that would interrogate the role of the designer in society – to serve the needs of humanity rather than to produce stylish work for market-driven forces. It did not take long for de Bretteville to begin questioning how and in what directions these motivations might transform graphic design.

An answer emerged after de Bretteville designed an issue of *Everywoman* newspaper for the artist group Miss Chicago and the California Girls, a product of the first Feminist Art Program, which had been established at Fresno State University in 1970 and headed by artist Judy Chicago. De Bretteville approached her supportive dean, Richard Farson, about establishing a Women's Design Program at CalArts, and the idea became manifest in 1971 with a class of fifteen.

With no model for what the programme might be, de Bretteville created an alternative to the dominant male attitudes reflected in the prevalent design of the day, which she described as 'the oversimplified, the unremittingly serious, the emphatically rational'.[1] In other words, she saw graphic design as a product of male-driven values and sought to reshape it around a different perspective – a feminist one. In opposition to design that was 'anonymous and authoritarian',[2] the Women's Design Program embraced values rejected by both modernist mores *and* contemporary society – the personal, the subjective and the domestic, alongside characteristics of complexity, ambiguity and contradiction.

Extending her reach beyond CalArts, de Bretteville in 1973 co-founded The Woman's Building with Judy Chicago and art historian Arlene Raven. In joining forces, the women provided a home for feminist organizations, and a space dedicated to the study and exploration of women's art, the display of work and shared activity. One of these in-house organizations, the Women's Graphic Center (also founded by de Bretteville), provided graphic-arts instruction, giving many women the skills needed to enter or advance within the job market.

Emigre magazine, no. 2, 1985

Feminism thus became a means – or, for my purposes, a tool – with which to interrupt conventionalized design. Long before 'participatory design' became a touchstone, de Bretteville upended the idea of a singular authority orchestrating a vision, instead seeing the designer as the facilitator of a collaborative process. As Lorraine Wild and David Karwan emphasize in their essay 'Agency and Urgency: The Medium and the Message',[3] de Bretteville, wielding feminism as a vital instrument, opened the door to values embraced and, today, taken for granted by designers and educators: working with communities, embracing the designer's voice, exploring new graphic languages and welcoming a multiplicity of views.

Tools for Self-Expression and Transformation

By the 1980s California was no longer a nonentity in the eyes of New Yorkers or the world. Its graphic design was now a design-press darling, admired and influential. There was West Coast punk; San Francisco's nostalgic eclecticism emblematized by three graphic designers nicknamed 'The Michaels' (Michael Cronan, Michael Manwaring and Michael Vanderbyl); the unleashing of graphic splashes, shapes and colour via April Greiman's California New Wave; and the pervasive California Memphis, created by Tamotsu Yagi for the Esprit clothing line. Coinciding front and centre was Apple and its '1984' commercial, promising a revolutionary future of personal freedom for all.

But while the world *finally* saw the light of a design sun rising in the west, graphic designers had mixed emotions about the sexy new tool getting so much attention. While bewitched by the audacious commercial and the potential of a newfangled device that could automate drudgery, they had trepidations about being replaced by a machine – or by office workers with their hands on its user-friendly desktop-publishing software. Yet if we go back to that other definition of a tool as a 'means to an end', we see California designers in the 1980s continuing to dictate new terms for design. Only now, unlike their predecessors (the ones who had paved the way), designers were operating *on* the radar, not under or off it.

In 1983 an essay by designer and educator Lorraine Wild, 'More than a few questions about graphic design education',[4] caused a rumble by confronting the state of graphic-design education at the time, which was mostly ragtag, inconsistently defined and usually took the form of a subset of classes in art programmes. The few programmes dedicated to graphic design were often stuck in the 1960s, teaching the supposedly timeless approach of Swiss-inspired modernism. Wild challenged her fellow educators to take a fresh look at graphic-design pedagogy as something beyond ad hoc skills or a particular style. Her essay caught the attention of Catherine Lord, dean of the School of Art at CalArts, who championed Wild's argument and hired her.

Arriving at CalArts in 1985, Wild joined a lineage of experimental graphic-design education tracing back to de Brettevilles' Women's Design

Program. With new hires, Ed Fella and Jeff Keedy, she set about radically transforming design education at undergraduate and graduate levels. They put concepts, meaning and aesthetic experimentation at the forefront. Classes cultivated discussion about the denotative and connotative meanings of images and how they might work in tandem with typography, rather than focusing only on formal criteria. Personal approaches, imagination and curiosity were encouraged, with the aim of connecting the individual designer to her work. Design history was seen as a continuum of change in which the current generation was participant, rather than as a fixed galaxy of stellar design luminaries. Any vestige of design as subservience, invested only in serving the communication needs of others, was banished; students were treated as equals in a community of artists. The programme that Wild, Keedy and Fella realized became a tool that transformed how graphic design was taught as well as how it was understood and practised. If the world looked different after 1985, it was in part because of Wild and her team.

By the 1990s software user-interface design emerged as a new challenge for graphic designers. Constrained by the palette of typefaces, colours and formats, and daunted by new demands for function, they felt adrift in unknown waters. Was this new realm even graphic design? User Interface (UI) and User Experience (UX) – terms and approaches originating from product and industrial design – challenged the domain to which this practice belonged, yet the interface was 'graphical' rather than mechanical. Graphic designers began to wonder whether their practice would absorb other disciplines or would itself be absorbed, given the complexities of this new reality.

But in the background, a new conversation about design was emerging along with new tools that confirmed California's special 'juju'. In the days before *Emigre* magazine, the design press rarely featured designers writing about graphic design. Those who did receive peer attention were uncritically celebrated as if they were gods. *Emigre* turned the tables. As Jeff Keedy points out in his essay reflecting on the history of the magazine – ironically titled 'Graphic Designers Probably Won't Read This, But ...'[5] – *Emigre* was the first publication to produce content written 'for, by, and about graphic designers ... "warts and all"'.[6]

The magazine's title reflected this outside-the-mainstream approach while nodding to its founders, three Dutch designers – émigrés themselves – living in San Francisco. Their ambition in starting *Emigre* in 1983 was to provide a venue for creative practitioners from around the world to share visual works and writing. In line with this experimental agenda, co-founder Rudy VanderLans enthusiastically designed the publication by seeing how far he could exploit the limited resources at his disposal. A year later – when Apple released the first friendly and somewhat affordable personal computer, and VanderLans and his wife Zuzana Licko (also a graphic designer) acquired a Macintosh 128K (a computer preceding the Mac) – Licko began to generate bold experiments in digital-font design that were soon incorporated into the magazine.

By 1987, with issue no. 8, the entrepreneurial magazine's typefaces and layouts were produced entirely with digital means. Two years later VanderLans (by then on his own, his partners having departed) decided to devote *Emigre*'s editorial direction entirely to a new conversation for design – provoked, in part, by the publication's unconventional and attention-getting approach to design. *Emigre* had recently been recognized by the prestigious *I.D. Annual Design Review* for 'pushing the boundaries', a tribute to Licko's digital fonts and VanderLans' layered, mis-registration and use of overprinting in layouts – techniques that once signalled sloppy production. Why not push the boundaries even further?

The intent was, in VanderLans' words, to feature 'designers whose work does not conform to mainstream ideas ... whose work is still developing ... [and] to provide a more complete picture of the state of graphic design.'[7] The dialogue he started became a tool that redirected the conversation about graphic design, expanding the scope of what kind of work was appreciated. *Emigre* forged a new generation of graphic-design readers, in particular designers giving serious consideration to what they were doing. It inspired controversy and debate, and challenged the status quo. Any fear of 'getting it wrong', by East Coast standards, diminished.

While *Emigre* tooled a new conversation for design, David Carson was forging a new typography that became a tool for reading – or, at least, reading blasted open. Gone was any remnant of legibility standards. The 'sacred line' of graphic design now crossed, Carson launched the first salvo in what became the design culture battle, with one camp known as the 'cult of the ugly', as represented by his design for the surfing magazine, *Beach Culture*. By the time he became founding art director in 1992 of *Ray Gun*, a music magazine, it was full-on graphic-design war, featuring a new generation on one side that saw reading as something other than a linear experience, no longer constrained by the 'old rules', whether upside down or layered, overprinted, scratched, with sizes splashed and scattered across the page. The reading experience itself now superseded content.

Graphic Design as Tool

The next digital tidal wave came in the new millennium, and graphic designers faced yet another unknown coming out of California. This time it took the form of social media and the platforms to facilitate the dissemination of content for a seemingly endless terrain of global creation and consumption. The perspective behind Steinberg's witty illustration of a single place being, or seeing itself as, the centre of the universe was now completely flipped on its head. And the graphic designer was no longer centre of the design universe. Anyone could do design. The tools of liberation – of political messages and personal ones – could be created and disseminated *by* anyone *to* anyone with a laptop or even, just a few years later, a smartphone. The Emory Douglas-crafted evocative and moving Black Panthers poster of yesteryear was now supplanted by the #blacklivesmatter hashtag.

Yet just as graphic design remained vital in the wake of the Apple Mac, the practice has expanded into new realms, genres and skills: interaction design, experience design, font design, web design, motion design and app design, just to name a very few. Graphic designers were forced to take stock and outline what kind of gravity held their field together, regardless of media or platform. Communicating with words and images; connecting, synthesizing and organizing ideas; working with narratives and complex systems; and deploying media to suit our ends – we were all creative spirits embodied in the pragmatics of knowing how to make things and make things happen.

What would the tools of design that had expanded the terrain so vitally be and mean now? Perhaps graphic design itself was the tool. Graphic design no longer uses tools but is itself a tool, a multipurpose instrument akin to the Swiss Army Knife, ready and able to tackle everything. No longer confined to workin' for the man from nine to five (in reality, nine to nine), we are now masters (or, my preference, mistresses) of our own universe. We certainly are no longer subject to constraints or definitions and, looking back, it all makes sense. California, after all, is the liberation birthplace. The golden coast, where the laws were loose and the edges soft, gave graphic design permission to break free from rote subservience and cookie-cutter modernism. And eventually, we didn't even need permission. We could just do.

Fully liberated from any constraints at all, designers have now launched their own organizations, enterprises and endeavours. Although not limited to California alone – and yet seemingly a vital birthplace – new forms of unfettered practice by graphic designers thrive on these sun-drenched shores. To name a few, in vast variety, Kate Johnson's Women's Center for Creative Work that she co-founded in 2013 to cultivate 'LA's feminist creative communities and practices';[8] films by Michael Polish of the Polish Brothers including the eerie production, *Twins Fall Idaho*, and those of Mike Mills who started out directing commercials for the Gap and recently wrote and directed the critically-acclaimed film *20th Century Women*; initiatives to better cities and the world, including Colleen Cocoran's co-development of CicLAvia, events that catalyze public spaces through car-free streets; and Matthew Manos's verynice, a practice that provides a model for socially responsible businesses; there are also graphic designers as retail and education entrepreneurs, such as Anna and Kirk Nozaki's shop Cattywampus, a curated wonderland of craft retail and classes; along with Chris Do and Jose Caballer's Skool, an enterprise that teaches business to creatives through video and workshops; and, just recently, Joe Potts, who launched Southland Institute, an alternative graphic design school.

While the rest of the world sought a common language and a common look, California graphic designers found new forms of political and personal expression brandishing unlikely graphic design tools in the form of rules, vernaculars, attitude, feminism, education, conversation and reading. And now, in turn, that graphic design is changing the world itself.

1 • SL de Bretteville, 'Some aspects of design from the perspective of a woman designer', *ICOGRAPHIC*, issue 6, 1973.
2 • *Ibid.*
3 • L Wild and D Karwan, 'Agency and Urgency: The Medium and the Message', in A Blauvelt (ed.), *Hippie Modernism: The Struggle for Utopia* (Minneapolis, 2015).
4 • L Wild, 'More than a few questions about graphic design education', *Design Journal*, vol. 1, no. 2 (1983).
5 • J Keedy, 'Graphic Designers Probably Won't Read This, But … ', in R VanderLans and Z Licko, *Emigre: Graphic Design into the Digital Realm* (New York, 1993).
6 • *Ibid.*
7 • R VanderLans and Z Licko, *Emigre: Graphic Design*

8 • Women's Center for Creative Work, 'About' (n.d.), <womenscenterforcreativework.com/about-2/>

Corita Kent, 'Power Up', 1965

In Los Angeles, pop art becomes political through the work of a practising nun.

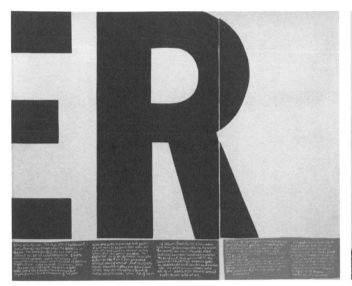
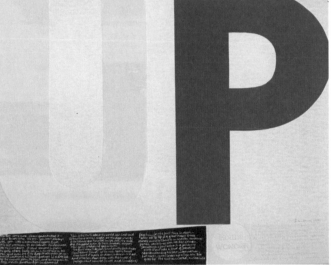

While teaching at Immaculate Heart College, Sister Corita Kent designs socio-political serigraphs that combine bold, bright imagery with provocative texts that she extracts from advertising slogans, street and grocery store signage, poetry, scripture, newspapers and magazines, philosophy and song lyrics. For 'Power Up', Kent borrows the slogan of Richfield Oil Corporation and marries it to a sermon by the activist priest Daniel Berrigan, transforming a gasoline ad into a statement on the empowering influence of the Word.

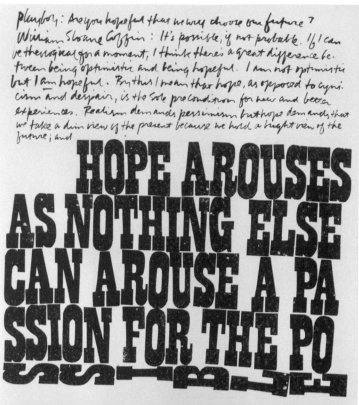

playboy: Are you hopeful that we will choose our future?
William Sloane Coffin: It's possible, if not probable. If I can be theological for a moment, I think there's a great difference between being optimistic and being hopeful. I am not optimistic but I am hopeful. By this I mean that hope, as opposed to cynicism and despair, is the sole precondition for new and better experiences. Realism demands pessimism but hope demands that we take a dim view of the present because we hold a bright view of the future; and

HOPE AROUSES AS NOTHING ELSE CAN AROUSE A PASSION FOR THE POSSIBLE

Corita Kent, 'A Passion for the Possible', 1969

Kent's screenprinted textual collages mobilize the secular and the religious, pop culture and fine art in order to ask philosophical questions about racism, poverty, military brutalities in Vietnam, and conflicts between radical and conservative positions within the Catholic Church.

Corita Kent, 'King's Dream', 1969

Emory Douglas, 'H. Rap Brown (Man with Match)', 1967

In Oakland, Emory Douglas gives form to black power.

From 1967 to 1980 Douglas oversees the art direction and production of *The Black Panther*, the party's official newspaper. As the party's Minister of Culture, Douglas establishes a visual language for the Black Panthers' message of resistance, empowerment and self-determination.

Emory Douglas, 'Afro-American solidarity with the oppressed people of the world', 1969

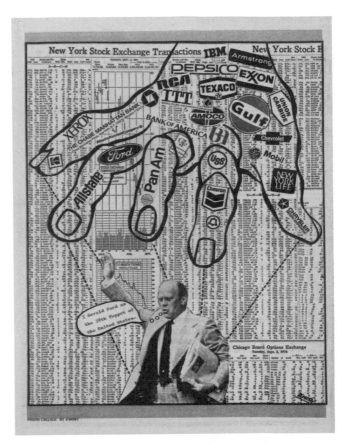

Emory Douglas, 'I Gerald Ford am the 38th puppet of the United States', 1974

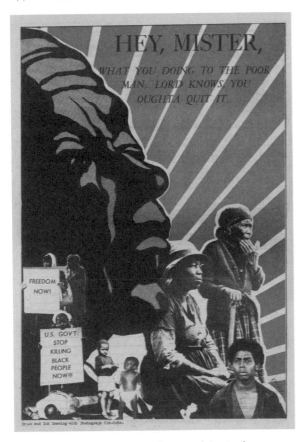

Emory Douglas, 'Hey, Mister, what you doing to the poor man, Lord knows, you oughta quit it', 1972

Emory Douglas, 'We shall survive. Without a doubt', 1971

Tools of Self-Expression and Rebellion   95

Shepard Fairey, 'We the People Are Greater than Fear', 2016

Protesters of Donald Trump's immigration order,
Los Angeles International Airport, 29 January 2017

Shepard Fairey, 'We the People Defend Dignity', 2016

The potential influence of activist design grows exponentially with the Internet. 'We the People', a poster series by graphic artist Shepard Fairey, leverages the power of digital distribution by making the posters' print files free to download and distribute.

Howard Harawitz, 'Free Speech Movement protestor, Berkeley', 1964

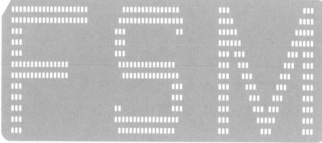

Free Speech Movement punch cards, 1964–5

California's tech industry informs its activism both in medium and message. As part of the Free Speech Movement, Berkeley-based students use punch cards to protest against the dangers of computers as technologies of dehumanization, centralized bureaucracy and war.

Fifty years later, the California chapter of the American Civil Liberties Union takes activism into the app store. Its Mobile Justice app allows users to record and report instances of police abuse and provides a reference guide for defending civil rights.

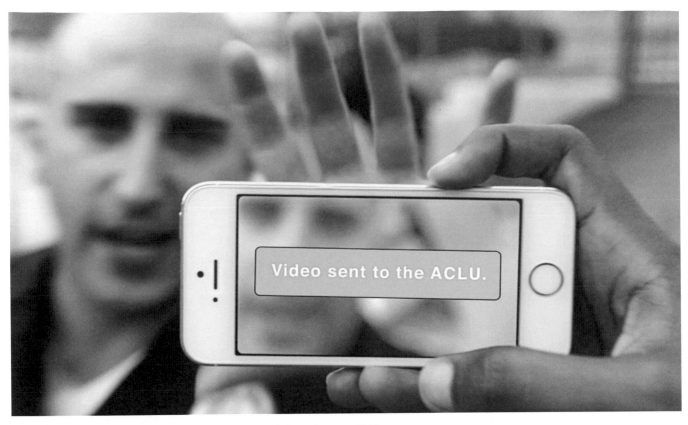

Smartphone video footage captured using the ACLU Mobile Justice app, 2015

RECORD

Film an incident by hitting RECORD, then simply tap the screen to stop. A copy of the incident will be automatically sent to the ACLU and saved to your Camera Roll.

After a recording ends, you will be prompted to fill out a short incident report. Bypass the incident report by simply pressing cancel; however, we encourage you to fill it out so we can learn more about what you saw.

Use the TEST button to ensure your camera is working without sending a video to the ACLU.

REPORT

Submit an incident report directly to the ACLU about an incident with law enforcement – or any other type of interaction with a government official – even if it was not recorded.

WITNESS

Enable push notifications in the SETTINGS tab, then hit WITNESS to get timely alerts when other users are recording a nearby incident. This allows communities to monitor and track law enforcement activity.

ALERTS

Enable push notifications and stay up-to-date on ACLU issues, campaigns and upcoming events in your community.

RIGHTS

Know your rights at the touch of a button, covering not only encounters with law enforcement but also everything from students' rights and health rights to free speech and the Bill of Rights itself.

MOBILEJUSTICE CA
EMPOWERED BY THE ACLU OF CALIFORNIA

You have the right to film law enforcement. MOBILE JUSTICE CA, a smartphone application empowered by the ACLU of California, makes it easier for community members to hold law enforcement agencies accountable for their actions.

DOWNLOAD FOR FREE & LEARN MORE: MOBILEJUSTICECA.ORG

GET IT ON Google play

Available on the App Store

ACLU Mobile Justice app promotional material, 2015

Despite its proximity to Silicon Valley, San Francisco's most influential piece of activist design is decidedly low tech. For the 1978 San Francisco Gay and Lesbian Parade, Gilbert Baker hand dyes and stitches the first rainbow pride flag. The design is inspired by Baker's admiration for the universality of the rainbow as a 'natural flag in the sky'.

Gilbert Baker, original eight-stripe Gay Pride flag, 1976

For a discriminating design organization specializing in Annual Reports, Brochures, Package Design, Direct Mail, Trademarks and completCorporate Identity Programs, call the BOSTON KLAN at either one of our Klaverns. In Los Angeles: 931-8751 or 931-8163. In Newport Beach: 540-4110.

BOSTON & BOSTON: EQUAL OPPORTUNITY DESIGNERS

Advertisement for Boston & Boston design agency, 1966

CHEERING OURSELVES

Sheila Levrant de Bretteville, *Everywoman* newspaper centrefold, 1970

California's culture of free expression includes the freedom to offend. To advertise his Los Angeles studio, Archie Boston creates a series of self-promotions that evoke and subvert America's racist history. At the California Institute of the Arts, Sheila de Bretteville designs a special issue of the feminist newspaper *Everywoman*. Its centrefold recreates the 'give me a C, give me a U, give me an N, give me a T' cheer used by students in de Bretteville's department.

April Greiman and Jayme Odgers, CalArts brochure, 1978

April Greiman and Jayme Odgers, *WET* magazine, no. 20, 1979

By the 1980s California's designers are in open rebellion against the orthodoxies of design itself.

Shortly after relocating to Los Angeles, the graphic designer April Greiman upends her rationalist training in favour of a hybrid, hyper-individualized multimedia style that she describes as 'the Swiss school on acid'.

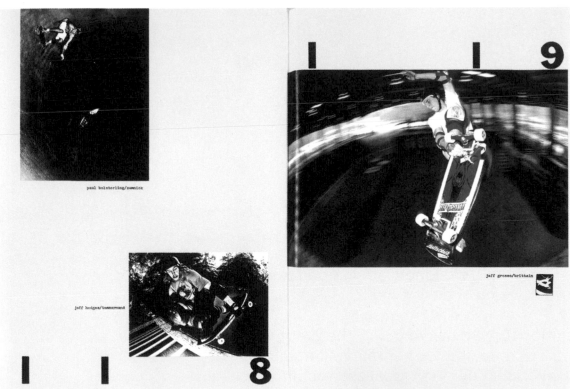

In the pages of *Transworld, Beach Culture* and *Ray Gun* magazines, David Carson projects an intensely personal graphic language that stretches the limits of legibility.

Top: David Carson, *Transworld* magazine, 'FULL BLEED' cover, 1985
Bottom: David Carson, *Transworld* magazine, 'FULL BLEED' interior, 1985

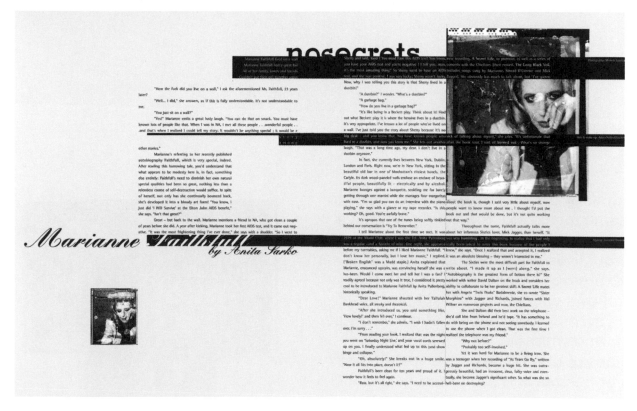

Top: David Carson, *Ray Gun* magazine, no. 25 cover, 1995
Bottom: David Carson, *Ray Gun* magazine, no. 25 interior, 1995

Tools of Self-Expression and Rebellion   107

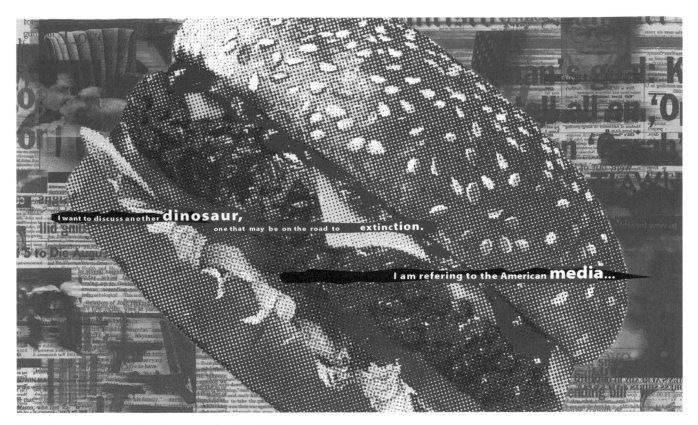

Erik Adigard, 'Mind Grenade', visual essay for *Wired*, 1993

Wired bursts into being in 1993. According to its issue one manifesto, the magazine exists 'because the digital Revolution is whipping through our lives like a Bengali typhoon'. *Wired*'s design expresses a similar sense of urgency: energized by a cacophony of typefaces streaking across post-psychedelic backdrops, the magazine embodies the multimedia possibilities of the digital convergence that *Wired* prophesizes and promotes.

John Plunkett, *Mind Grenades: Manifestos from the Future*, containing the first three years of *Wired* magazine's introductory statements, 1996

On the magazine cover:

WIRED

Wired Zero Issue
Soul of the Digital Age

The FTC's Secret Agenda to Dismantle Microsoft

Brit Hume What's Wrong With The Computer Press

34395

0 484957 5

04

John Perry Barlow
What a Long Strange Trip It's Been
The Wired Interview

John Plunkett and Barbara Kuhr, *Wired* magazine prototype, 1991

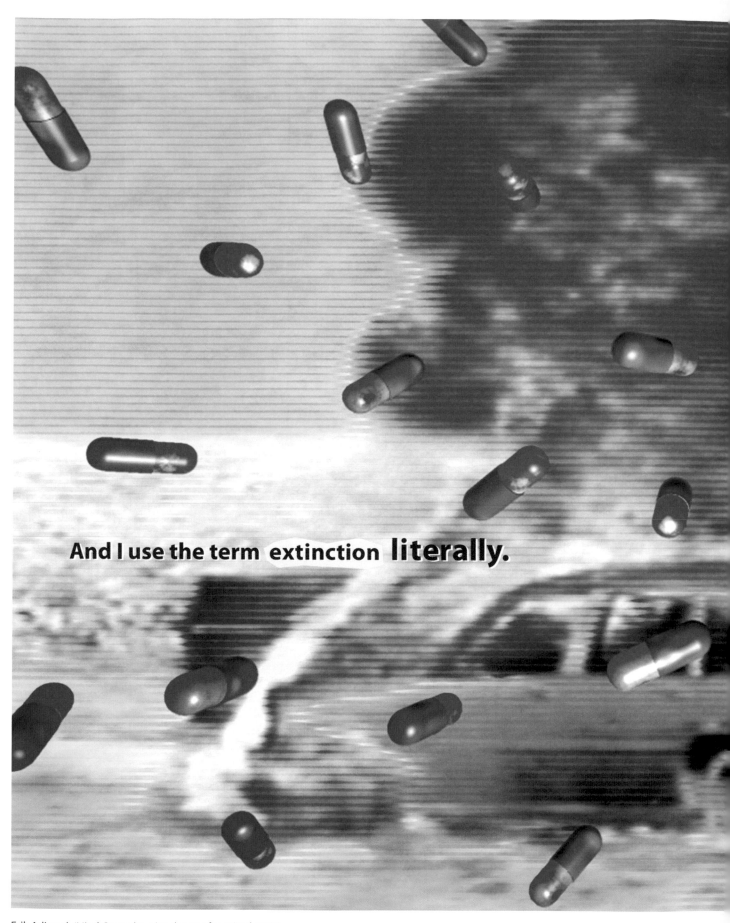

And I use the term extinction literally.

Erik Adigard, 'Mind Grenade', visual essay for *Wired*, 1993

Say What You Want

To my mind, it is likely that what we now understand as the mass media will be gone within ten years. Vanished, without a trace."

–Michael Crichton

With the arrival of mobile phone texting and social media, communication becomes even more concise – whenever possible, just a finger tap.

Originating on Japanese mobile phones in the late 1990s, emojis go global when Apple incorporates them into iOS 5. In a few years an initial library of just over 200 evolves into almost a thousand. We now speak in pictures.

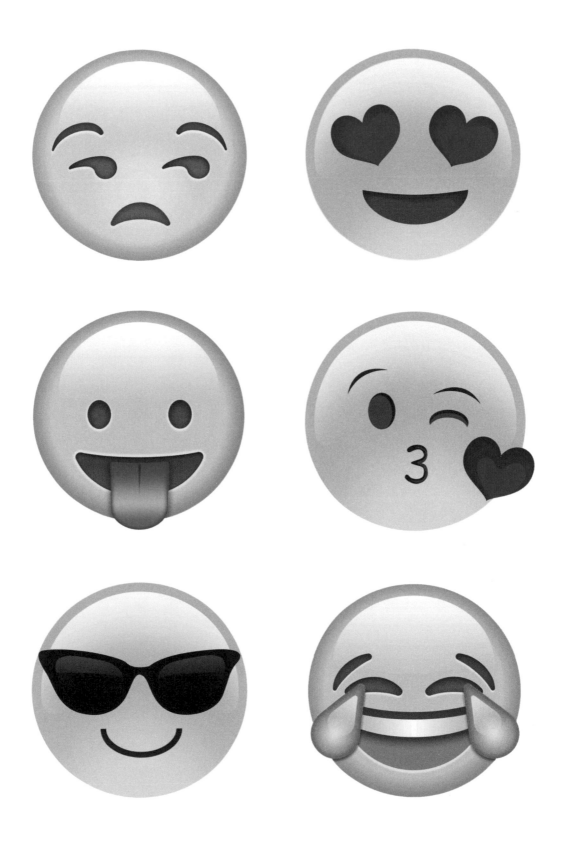

MAKE WHAT YOU WANT

Tools of Production and Self-Reliance

California has always placed a premium on personal autonomy, but with the commune movement of the 1960s and 1970s the pioneer spirit is revived. 'Access to tools' becomes a necessity. The same ethos fuels the personal computer revolution. The tools of the military-industrial complex are made available to the individual. Democratizing technology is almost a duty – and a profitable one. From desktop publishing to the Maker movement to biohacking, the amateur is king and 'do it yourself' is an imperative. Silicon Valley's start-up culture feeds on an ecosystem that can turn a DIY project into a global phenomenon in a matter of months.

MORE IS BETTER

Making Makers in California

BRENDAN McGETRICK

You too can be a designer

In his 2009 TED talk, Tim Brown, chief executive officer of the innovation consultancy IDEO, announced that 'design has become too important to be left to designers'.[1] It is an odd statement from the head of a design office. Taken in isolation, it could be read as a humble acknowledgement of a profession's limits, maybe even a cry for help. Tim Brown is British, and the talk took place in Oxford, so it's also possible that his remark reflects a cultural inclination towards understatement and self-deprecation. But I would argue that his statement is, in fact, quintessentially Californian. It expresses, in ten words, the defining features of that state's peculiar contribution to international design culture, particularly as it relates to the topic of making. It provides a context in which seemingly unrelated innovations such as the skateboard, genetic engineering and Frank Gehry's computer-assisted architecture make some kind of sense. As such, it's worth spending time unpacking the assumptions built into Brown's idea before going in search of their origins.

Assumption 1: Design, as a practice and process, is in a constant state of change.

In Silicon Valley, all technologies, relationships and business models exist in flux. The notion that anything has been finally figured out, can be ultimately relied on, or has been definitively mastered goes against the founding principles of the place. As Kevin Kelly, co-founder of *Wired*, has explained it, 'Because of technology everything we make is always in the process of becoming. Every kind of thing is becoming something else, while it churns from "might" to "is" … This never-ending change is the pivotal axis of the modern world.'[2]

Design is at the centre of this churn and, were he speaking to his California colleagues, I suspect that Brown would have applied more active, inspirational phrasing: Design *is becoming* too important … Before his mixed Oxford audience, though, the action is placed in the past, and the CEO acts as a reporter delivering an important bulletin from the front.

Assumption 2: Design is of infinite scope and unlimited value.

California is perhaps most famous for making things famous. Somewhere in its experimental, showbiz-centric, aggressively entrepreneurial culture is an aptitude for taking established ideas and enlarging them to Olympian scale.

For decades, designers have advocated greater influence over everything, 'from the spoon to the city', as Ernesto Rogers once put it.[3] This sentiment has been embraced, and radically expanded, in California. Not content with defining only the features of the physical world, Silicon Valley's designers now claim everything from income inequality to environmental justice as part of their purview.

As Brown himself explains in an essay for *Harvard Business Review*:

No matter where we look, we see problems that can be solved only through innovation:

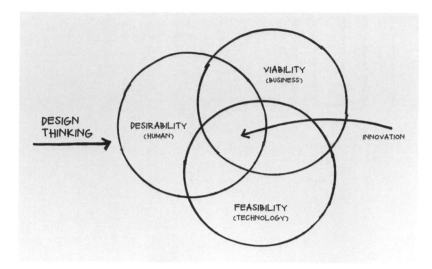

DESIGN THINKING →

DESIRABILITY (HUMAN)

VIABILITY (BUSINESS)

FEASIBILITY (TECHNOLOGY)

INNOVATION

Above: IDEO, Design Thinking diagram, 2008
Page 116: Steve Wozniak and Steve Jobs with the Apple I in Jobs's family garage, Palo Alto, 1976

unaffordable or unavailable health care, billions of people trying to live on just a few dollars a day, energy usage that outpaces the planet's ability to support it, education systems that fail many students, companies whose traditional markets are disrupted by new technologies or demographic shifts.[4]

These would not typically be considered design problems, but Brown is one of many in California working to convince clients that they actually are. He continues:

These problems all have people at their heart. They require a human-centered, creative, iterative, and practical approach to finding the best ideas and ultimate solutions. Design thinking is just such an approach to innovation.[5]

What is design thinking? 'Put simply,' Brown explains, 'it is a discipline that uses the designer's sensibility and methods to match people's needs with what is technologically feasible and what a viable business strategy can convert into customer value and market opportunity.'[6]
If that doesn't sound simple to you, you are not alone – and the diagram that IDEO provided to illustrate its CEO's ideas doesn't help much either. Put slightly more simply, Brown's TED Talk declaration means that design thinking is a belief system and a business model based on the idea that one does not have to be a designer to think like one. Without having natural aesthetic talents or

professional training, people from all backgrounds can become designers. This inclusiveness is essential to Silicon Valley's expanded definition of design. It is also the latest – and, in some ways, most radical – step in California's ongoing experiment in opening up industries to amateurs. It reveals the third assumption embedded in Brown's claim.

Assumption 3: Design works best when it makes elite tools accessible to all.
Design thinking comes predominantly from California, but it was not invented there.[7] Many essential components of its methodological toolkit – including user observation and interviewing, mind mapping and rapid prototyping – originated elsewhere. But it was in California that they were organized into a coherent programme and exposed to the public. This exposure – to anyone interested – is what makes design thinking quintessentially Californian. It assumes that more is better. More choices, more contributors. More brains working on more problems. It takes tools that were privately held, makes them public and invites everyone to try. In this sense, design thinking is simply the most abstract expression of the same culture that produced the personal computer, desktop publishing and the awe-inspiring, user-generated mess we call the Web.
It should come as no surprise that in a place as pragmatic and market-minded as California, design thinking transitioned instantaneously from an insight into an industry. An ever-expanding network of advocates now spans the globe,

advising governments, corporations, charities and educational institutions of all kinds. In 2004 Stanford University launched the Hasso Plattner Institute for Design, its so-called d.school, in order to 'support "students" of design thinking who range from kindergarteners to senior executives'.[8] In the years since, d.school has evolved into a machine for developing design thinkers and a model of the architectural and social environments best suited to the task. In 2012 two d.school professors released *Make Space*, a textbook for anyone interested in developing the kind of environments that are best suited to design thinking. The general ethos emphasizes adaptability: 'there's not just one ideal design for a collaborative space,' d.school co-founder David Kelley writes. 'The people using it should be able to transform it themselves, move things around, and create what they need for the work they're doing at the moment.'[9]

Perhaps unsurprising for a school in Silicon Valley, the d.school's designers express architectural ideas in the language of computer software. They encourage their colleagues to 'design for designers', rather than users, and to imagine their innovation space as an API, or application programming interface, the set of protocols that allows outside programmers to build applications onto platforms like Twitter, Google and Facebook. 'The job of a space designer is shifting,' they explain. 'Buzzwords notwithstanding – do-it-yourself, maker, participatory media, creator culture, this or that 2.0 – right now it is about empowering people to make and take action. Space design is particularly attuned to this goal.'[10]

'Space design' is d.school's usefully ambiguous phrase for a field that includes architectural, industrial, pedagogical and sociological strategies. If d.school is 'space design's' epicentre, its antecedents can be found throughout California – particularly among its research laboratories and garage workshops. Space design combines elements of each strategy to stimulate the intellectually curious, interdisciplinary atmosphere of a lab within the unfinished, hands-on environment of a garage.

The garage environment is particularly resource-rich for space designers. Its physical properties are important: 'expose raw materials,' *Make Space*'s authors advise, 'keep supplies and tools visible for inspiration and instruction.'[11] But equally significant is its symbolism. Silicon Valley itself started in a garage, or so the story goes. From 1938 to 1939, William Hewlett and David Packard experimented with various electronic devices in a one-car garage next to Packard's home. Their efforts eventually produced an audio oscillator that allowed them to launch Hewlett-Packard, now one of the world's largest technology companies. Since 1989 Packard's garage has been listed as a historical landmark, with a plaque in front declaring it the 'Birthplace of Silicon Valley'.[12]

Many of California's best-loved companies – including Apple, Google, Disney and the toy companies Mattel and Wham-O – have origin stories involving a garage. Their success suggests that all a would-be tycoon needs is talent, a marketable idea and a little bit of space. It's a beautiful notion, redolent of the best aspects of entrepreneurship, but it is largely fantasy. Research has shown that the garage itself is often a small part of the infrastructure needed for a successful start-up. 'The legend of the garage entrepreneur obscures a more central reality of entrepreneurship research,' Pino Audia and Chris Rider explain in 'A Garage and an Idea'. 'Many entrepreneurs acquire the psychological and social resources necessary to form new companies through prior experiences at existing organizations in related industries.'[13]

The story of Apple bears this out. According to legend, Steve Jobs and Steve Wozniak built the first hundred Apple I computers in the Jobs family home and garage in Los Altos. (Both house and garage are now protected landmarks.)[14] According to Wozniak, though, the garage didn't matter that much. In an interview with *Bloomberg*, the Apple co-founder described the story as a useful but misleading myth: 'The garage represents us better than anything else,' he explained, 'but we did no designs there … no breadboarding, no prototyping, no planning of products. We did no manufacturing there.' Where was the manufacturing done? 'The work was being done – soldering things together, putting the chips together, designing them, drawing them on drafting tables – at my cubicle at Hewlett-Packard in Cupertino.'[15]

When they started Apple, both Wozniak and Jobs had full-time jobs – at HP and Atari, respectively. In addition to equipment, these jobs gave them access to the psychological and social resources that Audia and Rider mention. Atari's founder Nolan Bushnell advised Jobs and introduced him to a venture capitalist who, in turn, introduced him to Mike Markkula, an angel investor in Apple and co-author of its first business plan. The first fifty Apple Is were sold to Paul Jay Terrell, owner of a computer store called The Byte Shop, whom Jobs and Wozniak met in a PC hobbyist group called the Homebrew Computer Club.[16]

All of these resources were available in the companies and communities around Los Altos and Cupertino. As enjoyable as it is to imagine two smart young guys side-by-side in a one-car garage building the basis of what would become the world's richest company, the story of Apple seems to confirm what every real-estate agent already knows: where the garage is matters more than who's in it.

Still, the Apple garage shouldn't be undervalued. It remains a potent symbol of what is possible, and a sacred site for start-ups of all kinds. Due in part to Apple's example, the dream of DIY manufacturing endures and, in many ways, today's hardware developers have it easier. Wozniak needed his job at HP to access the space and equipment required to make the Apple I. His descendants now have access to hundreds of public facilities that offer them superior tools, advice and even an identity.

You too can be a manufacturer

In May 2014, *Time* magazine published an opinion piece entitled 'Why the Maker Movement is important to America's future'. Written by a tech-industry analyst, the piece describes the movement as an extension of the grass-roots, garage-based hacker culture that produced Wozniak and Jobs.

'I was in Silicon Valley in the late 1970s,' the author explains, 'and I started to get more interested in the Homebrew Computer Club and similar user groups where people could get together and talk about tech-related interests. This was how I first got interested in computers.' A few lines later he adds, 'Fast forward to today, and I am very excited about the Maker Movement.'[17]

Maker Movement is an umbrella term for an informal network of people, places, tools, events and online resources that encourages the making of new things. These things range from Victorian-style bookmarks to synthetic biology, and its advocates insist that the movement is open to everyone.

In the opening chapter of his 2013 bestseller *Makers: The New Industrial Revolution*, Chris Anderson, former editor of *Wired*, states:

We are all Makers … It's not just about workshops, garages, and man caves. If you love to cook, you're a kitchen Maker and your stove is your workbench … If you love to plant you're a garden Maker. Knitting and sewing, scrapbooking, beading, and cross-stitching – all Making.[18]

But, as the title of Anderson's book implies, the Maker Movement isn't really about sewing or beading or any other pre-modern technology. It's about high technology: specifically, 3D printing and the Arduino electronic prototyping platform, CNC milling machines, laser cutters and other fabrication tools – all combined with an online infrastructure for the easy sourcing of parts and sharing of knowledge. It is this combination of the industrial and the online that makes Anderson's new industrial revolution possible.

What makes it Californian, I think, is the movement's insistence on access to tools as a fundamental human right. In *The Maker Movement Manifesto*, Mark Hatch writes:

The tools of the industrial revolution have been exceedingly expensive, hard to use, and of limited power – until now. They are now cheap, easy to use, and powerful, yet we have not made any changes to how we organize access to these tools. This must change.[19]

Hatch sees the solution in his own company, TechShop, as well as hundreds of similar organizations that offer space, high-end prototyping equipment and technical training to amateurs. These organizations take many forms, from loosely organized individuals to for-profit companies; non-profit corporations; and enterprises affiliated with schools, universities and public libraries. Participants in these makerspaces gain access to resources surpassing what almost any individual can afford or fit in a garage. They also become part of a community of Makers who – in an unplanned, open-source way – are constantly expanding the tools at their disposal. At this point, therefore, someone with interest and no experience needs very little to get started. The Maker community offers educational resources via websites, podcasts, YouTube channels, books and TV shows dedicated to DIY. It maintains repositories of open-source computer code, such as GitHub. The equipment and raw materials of desktop manufacturing are easily available in Maker shops, online and off. Funding for the most ambitious projects generally comes from the community via Indiegogo and a dozen other crowdsource sites. Finished works are distributed directly or sold on Etsy, Ebay or in offline shops specializing in Maker products.

This ecosystem is nourished by its members' enthusiasm. With each addition, the community reinforces and amplifies itself. At their most ardent, Makers present themselves as part of a resistance movement, struggling against the repressive impulses of industry. 'Revolutions are fought and won with arms,' Hatch writes in his Maker manifesto. 'Tools are our "arms". Without access to them, nothing has changed.'[20]

If this argument sounds familiar, it's probably because it was popularized by Steve Jobs. The dream of democratizing industry has deep roots in California, but Jobs was its most insistent advocate.

Maker space in Menlo Park, California, 2014

Apple based entire ad campaigns around the idea.[21] Over the years, the company contributed a number of important weapons to the Makers' arsenal, but its greatest remains the Macintosh, the so-called 'computer for the rest of us'.[22]

You too can be a publisher

In some ways, the Macintosh is an explicitly anti-Maker machine. From the start, it was designed to reduce its users' freedom to customize, upgrade and expand. Jef Raskin, the initiator of the project, originally described the Macintosh as a computer for a 'person in the street'. Frustrated with the intimidating adaptability of the Apple II, Raskin concluded that the person in the street would be better served by a complete and largely closed system.

'There were to be no peripheral slots so that customers never had to see the inside of the machine,' Raskin says of his initial concept. 'There was a fixed memory size so that all applications would run on all Macintoshes; the screen, keyboard, and mass-storage device (and, we hoped, a printer) were to be built-in so that the customer got a truly complete system, and so that we could control the appearance of characters and graphics.'[23]

Controlling the appearance of characters and graphics was essential, because the Macintosh was to be the first mass-market PC that had a graphical user interface (GUI). This GUI allowed users to communicate with the computer using a metaphorical desktop that included icons of real life items instead of abstract, textual commands.

As the technology journalist Steven Levy has explained, until that point, personal computers were locked in an esoteric realm of codes and commands. They looked unfriendly, with grainy, green letters glowing against a black screen. Even the simplest tasks required memorizing the proper commands, then executing several exacting steps.[24] The Macintosh was not the first PC to offer an alternative, but it was the first to make it affordable and, perhaps more importantly, lovable.

As Levy explains:

The Macintosh was friendly. It opened with a smile. Words appeared with the clarity of text on a printed page – and for the first time, ordinary people had the power to format text as professional printers did. Selecting and moving text was made dramatically easier by the then-quaint mouse accompanying the keyboard. You could draw on it. This humble shoebox-sized machine had a simplicity that instantly empowered you.[25]

Even before its release, the Macintosh's bitmapped screen was inspiring new forms of making. Many of its original icons, including the Mac's start-up smile, were designed by Susan Kare, a graphic designer and author of some of the first digital fonts. When Kare sketched the icons for the first Macintosh operating system in the early 1980s, she had only basic black-and-white pixels with which to create a universal user language. At a time when most designers were put off by the limitations of the computer and its inability

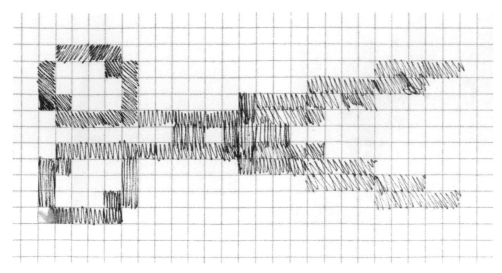

Susan Kare, sketch of the 'cut' pixel icon, designed for the original Mac OS, 1982

to exactly replicate existing technology, Kare was inspired by the digital environment, working within limitations as if they were assets.[26] Using graph paper, with one box equivalent to one pixel, Kare designed intuitive icons for various functions that a computer user might undertake (for example, a pair of scissors symbolized cutting text). These pictogram icons were designed to be an instinctive language that could be understood by users of all backgrounds in all places.[27]

Kare's efforts were soon echoed by the Macintosh's first users. For a certain class of artist and graphic designer, Apple's machine was more than a tool: it was a medium in itself. The LA-based designer April Greiman was an early adopter who explored the possibilities of digital imagery at a time when the Mac's technical limitations made the process exhausting.

In 1986 Greiman was commissioned to design an issue of *Design Quarterly* for the Walker Art Center. A year earlier, the combination of the Mac, Apple's LaserWriter printer and Mac-specific software like Aldus PageMaker had enabled users to design, preview and print page layouts complete with text and graphics – an innovation later known as desktop publishing.[28] Greiman's *Design Quarterly #133* took advantage of these new powers, and transformed the issue into an open question on what a magazine could be.

Instead of the magazine's standard sixteen-spread sequence, Greiman reformatted the piece as a poster that folded out to almost three by six feet (900 x 1800 mm). On the front was an image of Greiman's digitized body amid layers of interacting images and text. On the back, colourful, atmospheric, spatial video images were interspersed with comments and painstaking notations on the digital process – a virtual landscape of text and image.[29]

Today, this all sounds simple enough – but Greiman's collage, entitled 'Does it Make Sense?', was an astounding technical feat at the time. In 1986 the process of integrating digitized video images and bitmapped type required a degree of patience and craft more commonly associated with pre-digital times. Greiman built the collage on the computer and outputted letter-sized pages on her dot-matrix machine, then directed the magazine's printer to assemble the pages and photograph the entire composition. The files were so large and the equipment so slow that Greiman would send the file to print as she left the studio in the evening, and it would be finishing when she returned in the morning.[30]

With its one megabyte of RAM and monochrome nine-inch (230 mm) display, it isn't hard to understand why many designers initially resisted the Macintosh. Those who didn't, however, gained a previously unthinkable amount of control over everything from format to layout to type. The magazine that took best advantage of these new freedoms was Berkeley-based *Emigre*. Founded in 1984, just before the release of the first Mac, *Emigre* quickly became a forum for designers interested in experimentation and technology. It featured in-depth articles and visual essays, in layouts that broke all rules – with varying type sizes, overlapping layers, text columns crashing

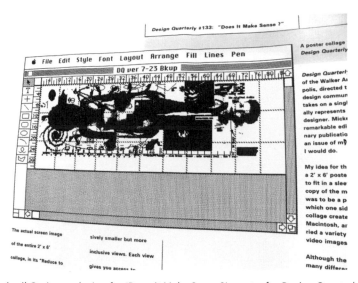

April Greiman, design for 'Does it Make Sense?', poster for *Design Quarterly*, no. 133, 1986

into each other and distorted letterforms (all techniques that the Macintosh made easier).[31]

Working with a bitmap font tool, *Emigre* co-founder Zuzana Licko created fonts for the magazine. Her Emperor, Oakland and Emigre fonts were designed as coarse bitmapped faces to accommodate low-resolution printer output. They were used in *Emigre* no. 2 and, after several readers inquired about their availability, the magazine began running ads for them in the third issue. Licko and her partner Rudy VanderLans then used proceeds from font sales to fund the magazine, allowing it to run ad-free.[32]

As former *Emigre* contributor Michael Dooley has observed, Brian Eno's quip about the Velvet Underground – that only a few thousand people bought their records but every one of them went on to form a band – could apply as well to *Emigre*. Although the print run of the first issue was 500 copies and its circulation peaked at 7,000, its reverberations are still being felt around the world. The magazine that VanderLans published and art directed, and the fonts Licko developed for it, have stimulated designers to defy, and even overthrow, entrenched rules and to set new standards.[33]

For Jobs and his compatriots in the tech community, the standards-destroying, individual-empowering, industry-disrupting implications of desktop publishing were the whole point. *Emigre*'s typographic and editorial iconoclasm was a small but powerful example of their belief in personalized technology as a source of radical change.

In hindsight, the idea that computers can empower individuals and create new communities seems obvious. But, as Fred Turner and others have observed, imagining the fruits of the military-industrial complex as tools of personal liberation was in itself a kind of revolution. For young Americans witnessing their emergence in the 1960s, computers loomed as technologies of dehumanization; centralized bureaucracy; and, ultimately, the Vietnam War.[34] The effort to undo these associations took decades and required thousands of contributors. Jobs was the most visible, but his inspiration came from Stewart Brand and his 'make what you want' manifesto, the *Whole Earth Catalog*.

You too can be a god

As Jobs would describe it decades later, the *Whole Earth Catalog* was 'like Google in paperback form'.[35] Originally created to help hippies find the tools they needed to build their own communes, the *Catalog* included everything from the fringed deerskin jackets and geodesic domes favoured by the communards to the cybernetic writings of Norbert Wiener and the latest calculators from Hewlett-Packard.[36] In later editions, alongside such supplies, Brand published letters from high-technology researchers next to first-hand reports from rural hippies.

Sized somewhere between a tabloid newspaper and a glossy magazine, divided into seven categories, the *Whole Earth Catalog* offered a cacophony of artefacts, voices and visual design. Decades before *Emigre* would label itself 'the magazine that ignores boundaries',[37] the *Catalog*

Emigre magazine, no. 19, 1991

provided a place where home-weaving kits and potters' wheels banged up against reports on the science of plastics and books on computer-generated music.[38] As Turner has described it, the *Catalog* presented these things within a design framework that echoed the frontier preoccupations of the back-to-the-land movement and the psychedelic design inclinations of the contemporary alternative press. Each page featured multiple typefaces, many seemingly created in the nineteenth century. They appeared on plain, rough paper – the tactile antithesis of the glossy magazine. Like its choice of products, the *Catalog*'s design mingled the psychedelic, the nostalgic and the practical.[39]

Like its audience, the *Catalog* celebrated small-scale technologies as ways for individuals to improve their lives. But it also offered up those tools, and itself, as prototypes of a new relationship between the individual, information and technology.[40] For Brand, the *Catalog* was a tool for readers, but the readers were tools too. They could write in and use the pages of the *Catalog* to tell one another about their experiences with particular products. They could learn of ongoing grass-roots projects and contact one another to join in. Anticipating the Maker Movement's user-generated online ecosystem, the *Catalog* and its quarterly *Supplement* revealed to their readers an emerging DIY world in which all could potentially participate.

On the inside cover of every edition, Brand launched the *Catalog* with a mini manifesto:

We are as gods and might as well get good at it. So far, remotely done power and glory – as via government, big business, formal education, church – has [sic] succeeded to the point where gross defects obscure actual gains. In response to this dilemma and to these gains a realm of intimate, personal power is developing – power of the individual to conduct his own education, find his own inspiration, shape his own environment, and share his adventure with whoever is interested.

These ideals still shape much of what is made in California. They ennoble everything from home-made skate videos to Frank Gehry's experiments with chain-link fencing and other cheap materials in his Santa Monica residence. They explain the impulse behind Tim Brown's claim that design is too important to be left to designers, and his conclusion that everyone should design. *We are as gods* – written in earnest, with the assumption that an unlimited supply of amateurs can accomplish more than all of the world's experts. To those who motivate, connect and control the content produced by these amateurs go the profits and the power. It is a rarified group, concentrated in California but open to anyone – or so they make it seem.

1 • T Brown, 'Tim Brown: Designers – think big!', video file (July 2009), <ted.com/talks/tim_brown_urges_designers_to_think_big>

2 • K Kelly, *The Inevitable: Understanding the 12 Technological Forces that Will Shape our Future* (New York, 2016), 6.

3 • Ernesto Rogers created the slogan 'Dal cucchiaio alla città' (From the spoon to the city) in 1952 in the Athens Charter, the manifesto of CIAM (the Congrès Internationaux d'Architecture Moderne).

4 • T Brown, 'Design Thinking', *Harvard Business Review* (June 2008), <hbr.org/2008/06/design-thinking>

5 • *Ibid.*

6 • *Ibid.*

7 • As Barry Katz explains in his design history of Silicon Valley, *Make It New*, the genealogy of 'Design Thinking' has become an academic cottage industry. Its origins lie arguably in the Ulm Model, developed by Horst Rittel and his colleagues at the Hochschule für Gestaltung and imported by Rittel to the Design Methods Group at the University of California at Berkeley in the early 1960s.

8 • 'Innovators, Not Innovations', (24 November 2016), <dschool.stanford.edu/our-point-of-view>

9 • S Doorley and S Witthoft, *Make Space: How to Set the Stage for Creative Collaboration* (Hoboken, New Jersey, 2012), 5.

10 • *Ibid.*, 236.

11 • *Ibid.*, 11.

12 • P Audia and C Rider, 'A Garage and an Idea: What More Does an Entrepreneur Need?' *California Management Review*, vol. 48, no. 1. (Fall 2005), 14–15.

13 • *Ibid.*, 7.

14 • J Green, 'Jobs house added as "historic resource"', *Mercury News* (28 October 2013), <mercurynews.com/2013/10/28/jobs-house-added-as-historic-resource>

15 • B Lisy, 'Steve Wozniak on Apple, the Computer Revolution, and Working With Steve Jobs', *Bloomberg* (4 December 2014), <bloomberg.com/news/articles/2014-12-04/apple-steve-wozniak-on-the-early-years-with-steve-jobs>

16 • Walter Isaacson describes the circumstances around the creation of the Apple I in detail in his biography *Steve Jobs* (New York, 2011).

17 • T Bajarin, 'Why the Maker Movement Is Important to America's Future', *Time* (19 May 2014), <time.com/104210/maker-faire-maker-movement>

18. C Anderson, *Makers: The New Industrial Revolution*, (New York, 2012), 13.

19 • M Hatch, *The Maker Movement Manifesto: Rules for Innovation in the New World of Crafters, Hackers, and Tinkerers* (New York, 2012), 30.

20 • *Ibid.*, 26.

21 • In particular, Apple's iconic '1984' advertisement for the launch of the Macintosh.

22 • In 1984 the Macintosh was marketed as 'the computer for the rest of us' in print and television advertisements.

23 • O Linzmayer, *Apple Confidential 2.0: The Definitive History of the World's Most Colorful Company* (San Francisco, 1999), 86.

24 • S Levy, 'The Macintosh is thirty and I was there for its birth', *Wired* (24 January 2014). <wired.com/2014/01/macintosh-30th-anniversary>

25 • *Ibid.*

26 • Alex Soojung-Kim Pang, Interview with Susan Kare, 'Making the Macintosh', Stanford University (8 September 2000) <web.stanford.edu/dept/SUL/sites/mac/primary/interviews/kare/index.html>

27 • P Antonelli and MM Fisher, 'Is This for Everyone? New Design Acquisitions at MoMA', *Inside/Out* (4 March 2015), <moma.org/explore/inside_out/2015/03/04/is-this-for-everyone-new-design-acquisitions-at-moma>

28 • M Spring, *Electronic Printing and Publishing: The Document Processing Revolution* (New York, 1991), 125–6.

29 • April Greiman biography, The American Institute of Graphic Arts (1998), <aiga.org/medalist-aprilgreiman>

30 • *Ibid.*

31 • J Clifford, 'Icons of Digital Design', *Smashing* (3 October 2014), <smashingmagazine.com/2014/10/icons-of-digital-design>

32 • M Dooley, 'Critical Conditions: Zuzana Licko, Rudy VanderLans, and the Emigre Spirit', *Graphic Design USA*, 18 (New York, 1998), <emigre.com/Editorial.php?sect=3&id=8>

33 • *Ibid.*

34 • F Turner, *From Counterculture to Cyberculture: Stewart Brand, the Whole Earth Network, and the Rise of Digital Utopianism* (Chicago, 2006).

35 • '"You've got to find what you love," Jobs says', prepared text of the Commencement address delivered by Steve Jobs, CEO of Apple Computer and of Pixar Animation Studios (12 June 2005), <news.stanford.edu/2005/06/14/jobs-061505>

36 • Turner, *Counterculture to Cyberculture*.

37 • K FitzGerald, 'Seeing and Reading: A Viewer's Guide to Periodic Literature', *Emigre in Norfolk* (Norfold, VA, 2005), <emigre.com/Editorial.php?sect=3&id=7>

38 • Turner, *Counterculture to Cyberculture*.

39 • *Ibid.*

40 • *Ibid.*

Stewart Brand, *Whole Earth Catalog*, no. 1, 1968

In 1968 Stewart Brand founds the *Whole Earth Catalog*. Part magazine, part mail order outlet, the *Catalog* becomes an essential resource for California's rapidly spreading counterculture communities. Under the slogan 'access to tools', the *Catalog* creates a community in print where back-to-the-land homesteaders, acid test graduates and innovators in architecture, science and technology make first contact.

Among other things, the *Catalog* is a reference for new forms of shelter, sustainable design and experimental community practices. It generates a number of more specialized spinoffs, including *Domebook One* and *Domebook Two*, manuals on do-it-yourself geodesic dome construction produced by *Catalog* co-editor Lloyd Kahn.

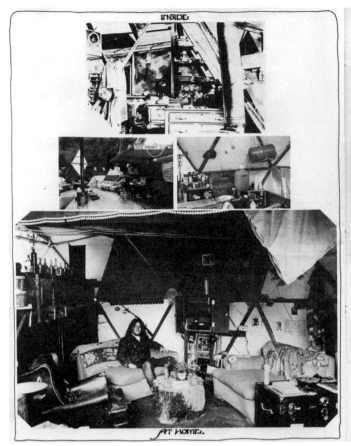

Lloyd Kahn, *Domebook*, no. 2, 1971

The Domebooks draw from the work of visionary polymath R Buckminster Fuller. Fuller's patented geodesic dome designs embody the architect's 'doing more with less' principle by enclosing the largest volume of interior space with the least amount of surface area, thus saving on materials and cost.

As a speaker and designer, Fuller is an inspiration to Stewart Brand and the *Whole Earth* network. Lightweight, durable and easy to construct, Fuller's geodesic domes become favoured housing on hippy communes throughout California.

Following spread: Buckminster Fuller and Chuck Byrne, construction visuals of Geodesic Dome, 1951

Fig. 4

Fig. 18b

Fig. 18a

Fig. 6

Fig. 5

Fig. 10

Fig. 13

Fig. 9

20

21

21

22

20

21

21

21

21

53

49

54

47

14

48

49

48

49

48

57

58

59

57

47

14

47

27

32

34

Ant Farm, 'Clean Air Pod' performance with Andy Shapiro and Kelly Gloger, University of California, Berkeley, 1970

Ant Farm, *Inflatocookbook*, 1971

Make What You Want

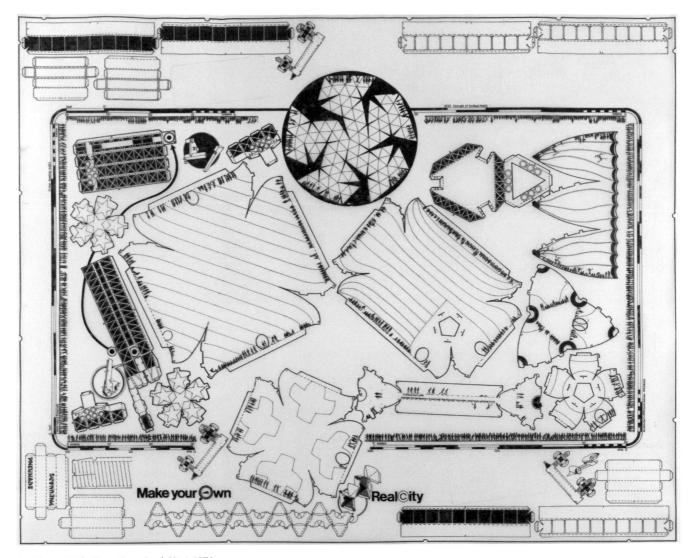

Ant Farm, 'Make Your Own Real City', 1973

As Buckminster Fuller's geodesic domes proliferate, the architecture collective Ant Farm develops inflatable structures that encompass vast volumes without substance. Instant buildings, these air-filled 'pillows' serve as transitory settings for happenings that seduce their participants into acting spontaneously.

Disney: the garage of Walt Disney's uncle, Garden Grove

Apple: the garage of Paul and Clara Jobs, Palo Alto

As California's designers imagine radical new forms of shelter, its entrepreneurs exploit what already exists. The suburban garage, an essential element of postwar housing throughout California, is transformed into a launch pad for billion-dollar businesses. Many of California's best-loved companies, including HP, Apple, Google, Disney, Hobie Surfboards, and the toy companies Mattel and Wham-O, get their starts in a garage.

HP: the garage of David and Lucille Packard, Palo Alto

Google: the garage of Susan Wojcicki, Menlo Park

The success of California's garage start-ups suggests that all an entrepreneur needs is talent, a marketable idea and some space. The truth is more complicated.

Silicon Valley's start-ups are embedded in a vast ecosystem of investors, universities, incubators, governmental bodies, billion dollar companies, media organizations, mentorship programs, lawyers and highly motivated kids capable of taking an entrepreneur's idea from pipe dream to IPO. This ever-intensifying, self-enriching ecosystem is the envy of the world and arguably Silicon Valley's greatest invention.

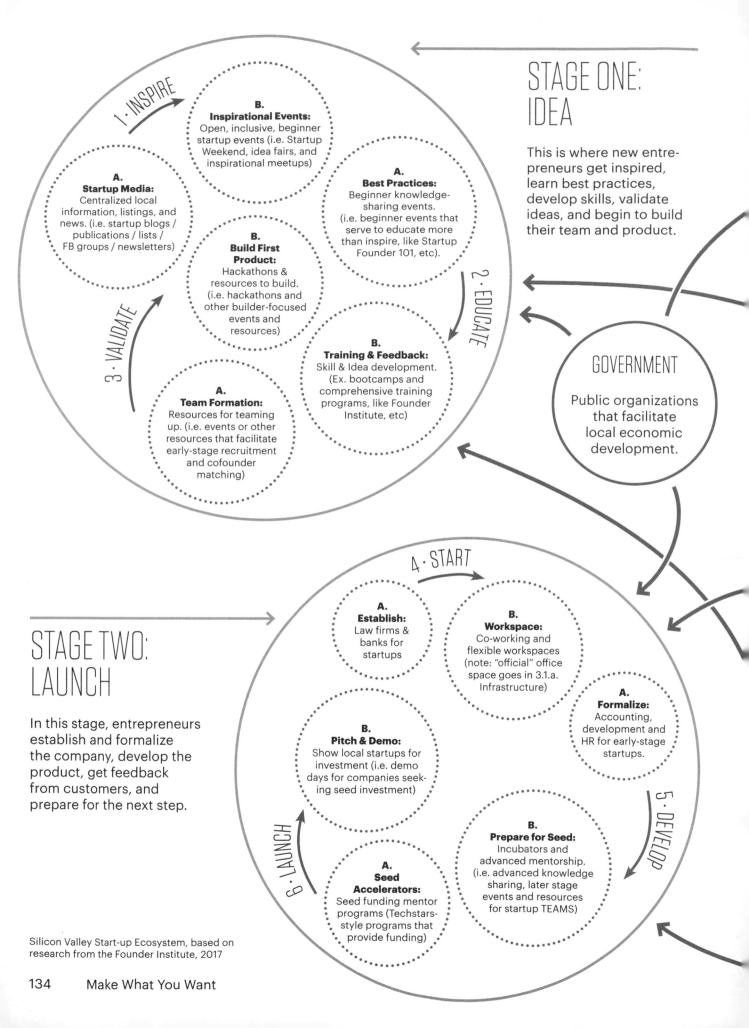

STAGE ONE: IDEA

This is where new entrepreneurs get inspired, learn best practices, develop skills, validate ideas, and begin to build their team and product.

1 · INSPIRE

B.
Inspirational Events:
Open, inclusive, beginner startup events (i.e. Startup Weekend, idea fairs, and inspirational meetups)

A.
Startup Media:
Centralized local information, listings, and news. (i.e. startup blogs / publications / lists / FB groups / newsletters)

A.
Best Practices:
Beginner knowledge-sharing events. (i.e. beginner events that serve to educate more than inspire, like Startup Founder 101, etc).

2 · EDUCATE

B.
Build First Product:
Hackathons & resources to build. (i.e. hackathons and other builder-focused events and resources)

B.
Training & Feedback:
Skill & Idea development. (Ex. bootcamps and comprehensive training programs, like Founder Institute, etc)

3 · VALIDATE

A.
Team Formation:
Resources for teaming up. (i.e. events or other resources that facilitate early-stage recruitment and cofounder matching)

GOVERNMENT

Public organizations that facilitate local economic development.

STAGE TWO: LAUNCH

In this stage, entrepreneurs establish and formalize the company, develop the product, get feedback from customers, and prepare for the next step.

4 · START

A.
Establish:
Law firms & banks for startups

B.
Workspace:
Co-working and flexible workspaces (note: "official" office space goes in 3.1.a. Infrastructure)

A.
Formalize:
Accounting, development and HR for early-stage startups.

B.
Pitch & Demo:
Show local startups for investment (i.e. demo days for companies seeking seed investment)

B.
Prepare for Seed:
Incubators and advanced mentorship. (i.e. advanced knowledge sharing, later stage events and resources for startup TEAMS)

5 · DEVELOP

6 · LAUNCH

A.
Seed Accelerators:
Seed funding mentor programs (Techstars-style programs that provide funding)

Silicon Valley Start-up Ecosystem, based on research from the Founder Institute, 2017

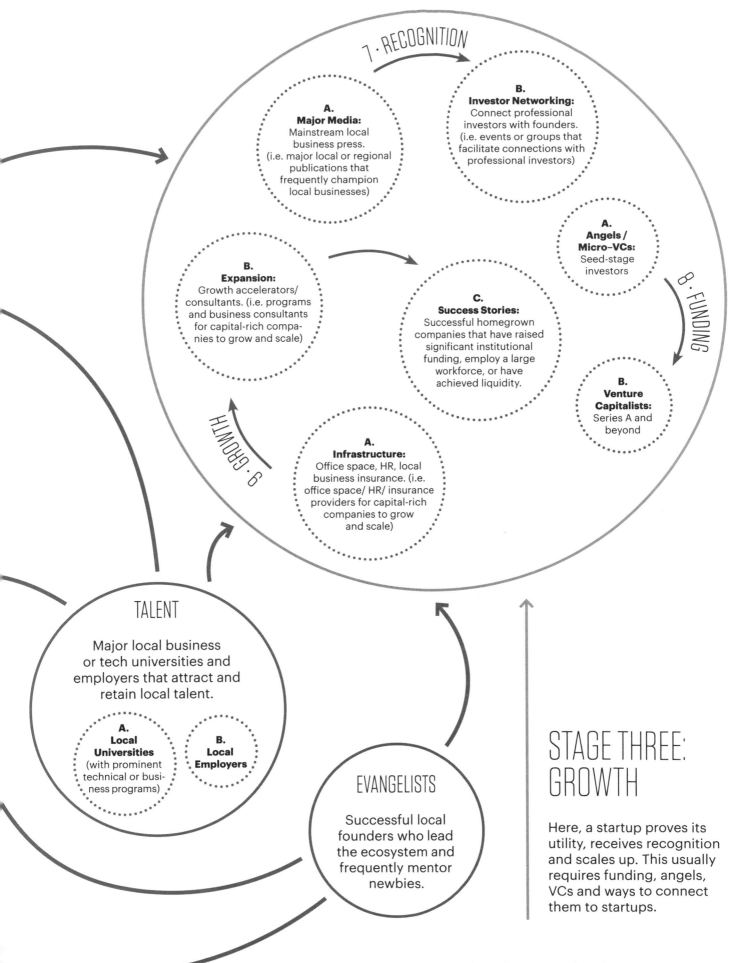

7 · RECOGNITION

**A.
Major Media:**
Mainstream local
business press.
(i.e. major local or regional
publications that
frequently champion
local businesses)

**B.
Investor Networking:**
Connect professional
investors with founders.
(i.e. events or groups that
facilitate connections with
professional investors)

**A.
Angels /
Micro-VCs:**
Seed-stage
investors

**B.
Expansion:**
Growth accelerators/
consultants. (i.e. programs
and business consultants
for capital-rich compa-
nies to grow and scale)

**C.
Success Stories:**
Successful homegrown
companies that have raised
significant institutional
funding, employ a large
workforce, or have
achieved liquidity.

8 · FUNDING

**B.
Venture
Capitalists:**
Series A and
beyond

9 · GROWTH

**A.
Infrastructure:**
Office space, HR, local
business insurance. (i.e.
office space/ HR/ insurance
providers for capital-rich
companies to grow
and scale)

TALENT

Major local business
or tech universities and
employers that attract and
retain local talent.

**A.
Local
Universities**
(with prominent
technical or busi-
ness programs)

**B.
Local
Employers**

EVANGELISTS

Successful local
founders who lead
the ecosystem and
frequently mentor
newbies.

STAGE THREE:
GROWTH

Here, a startup proves its
utility, receives recognition
and scales up. This usually
requires funding, angels,
VCs and ways to connect
them to startups.

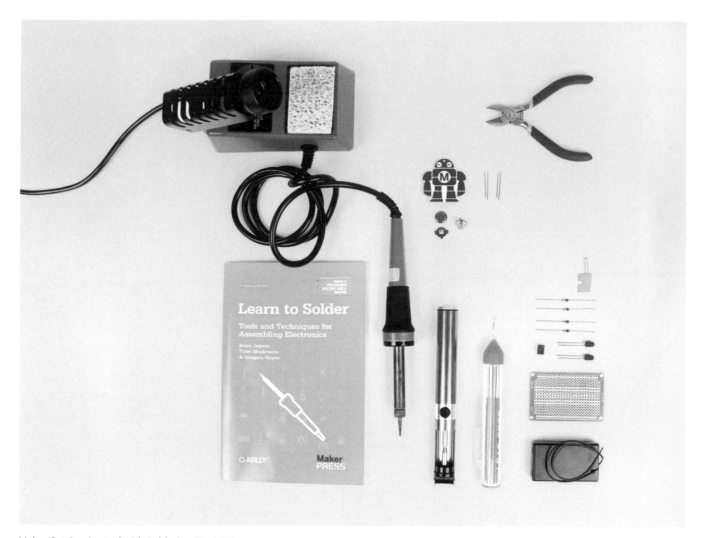

Make: Getting Started with Soldering Kit, 2016

With the launch of *Make* magazine and its Maker Faire, the garage-based hacker culture that produced Apple and various other Silicon Valley start-ups spreads worldwide. This Maker Movement is another kind of ecosystem, composed of people, places, tools, events and online resources dedicated to the DIY manufacture of everything from Victorian bookmarks to synthetic biology.

Make: Getting Started with Raspberry Pi Kit, 2016

THE MAKER'S BILL OF RIGHTS

- Meaningful and specific parts lists shall be included.
- Cases shall be easy to open. ■ Batteries shall be replaceable. ■ Special tools are allowed only for darn good reasons. ■ Profiting by selling expensive special tools is wrong, and not making special tools available is even worse. ■ Torx is OK; tamperproof is rarely OK.
- Components, not entire subassemblies, shall be replaceable. ■ Consumables, like fuses and filters, shall be easy to access. ■ Circuit boards shall be commented.
- Power from USB is good; power from proprietary power adapters is bad. ■ Standard connectors shall have pinouts defined. ■ If it snaps shut, it shall snap open. ■ Screws better than glues. ■ Docs and drivers shall have permalinks and shall reside for all perpetuity at archive.org. ■ Ease of repair shall be a design ideal, not an afterthought. ■ Metric or standard, not both.
- Schematics shall be included.

Make:
technology on your time

Drafted by Mister Jalopy, with assistance from Phillip Torrone and Simon Hill.

'The Maker's Bill of Rights', *Make* magazine, 2006

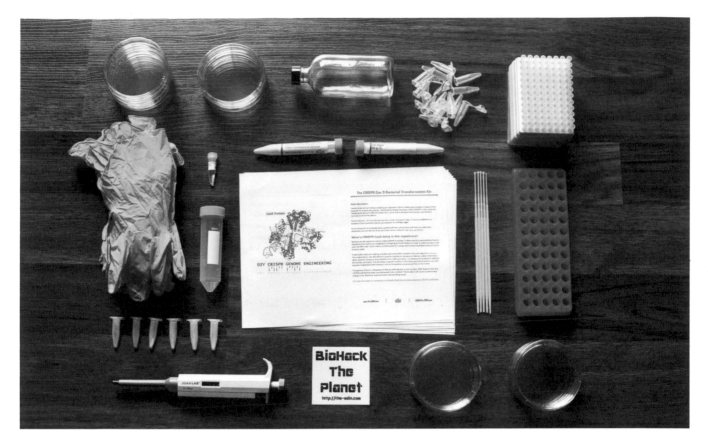

The ODIN, DIY Bacterial Gene Engineering CRISPR Kit, 2015

The next frontier in the Maker Movement is biohacking. DIY gene editing kits created by Castro Valley start-up The ODIN give amateurs the ability to engineer their own species.

Meanwhile, California's software giants engineer tools of their own. Genetic Constructor is a DNA-editing software created to empower scientists to design and manufacture living things. Produced by Autodesk, Genetic Constructor marks an inflection point where the tools of computer-assisted architectural design migrate from urban to biological systems.

Autodesk, Molecule Viewer web-based 3D visualization tool, 2017

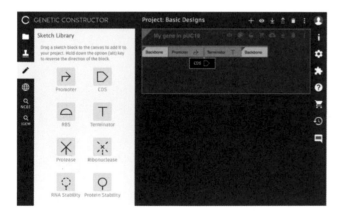

Autodesk, Genetic Constructor open-source biological design tool, 2017

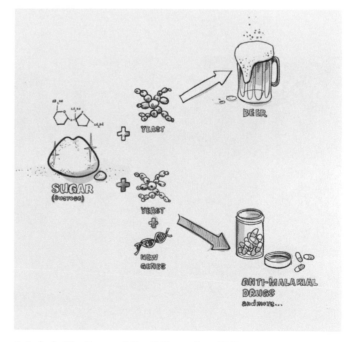

Autodesk, 'The Power of Yeast' illustration, 2017

Tools of Production and Self-Reliance 139

Frank Gehry, Gehry Partners, Walt Disney Concert Hall, completed 2003

Frank Gehry, Gehry Residence, 1978

Gehry Partners' CATIA model of the Walt Disney Concert Hall, 2001

Frank Gehry's exuberant experiments with architectural form are impossible without CAD. In the 1990s, while many of his peers are ignoring computers altogether, Gehry pioneers a new form of digital design by using software to optimize his architectural drawings and translate them directly into a process of fabrication and construction.

The resulting works, including the Disney Concert Hall in Los Angeles, are created using a customized version of CATIA, a CAD program originally developed for designing fighter jets. These digital tools allow Gehry to radically expand the experiments in material and form that he started years earlier in the analogue design of his home in Santa Monica.

Promotional photograph for Xerox Star workstation, 1981

Computer-assisted design starts at Xerox PARC. The company is founded in 1970 as a division of Xerox Corporation, and by the early 1980s it has produced many of the technologies that will define the computer as we know it. The bitmapped display, windows-based graphical user interface, desktop metaphor, mouse and printing all come from PARC's Palo Alto laboratories.

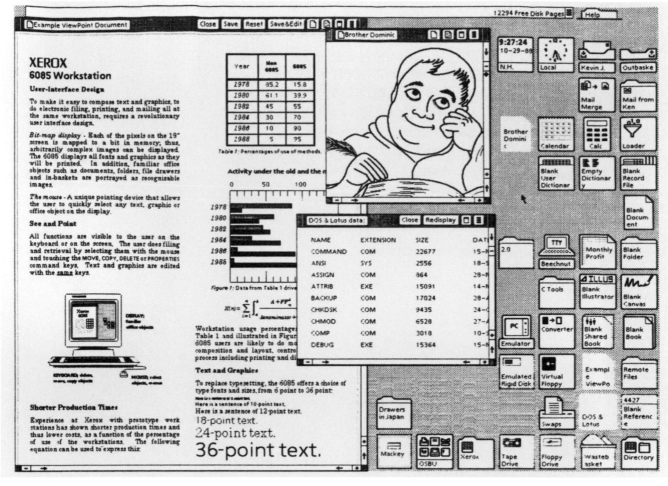

The Xerox Star's bitmapped graphical user interface, undated

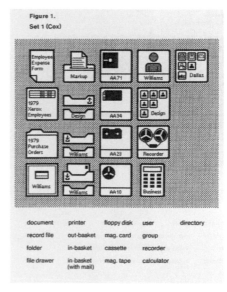

The Xerox Star's bitmapped graphical user interface, undated

In 1981 Xerox combines these innovations in its Star workstation and, in the process, invents an entirely new field: user interface design. The workstation represents a quantum leap for personal computing, but it is a commercial failure. It is not until Apple releases its Macintosh, the world's first mass-market PC with a graphical user interface and mouse, that the Star's potential is realized.

The Macintosh makes the computer truly personal.

Marketed as 'the computer for the rest of us', it applies the Star's desktop metaphor and adds a layer of emotion. Users starting up the Macintosh are greeted by a smiley Mac, part of a family of icons created by graphic designer Susan Kare. Kare's icons make previously arcane computer commands for cutting, saving and deleting easy to understand and fun to execute.

The Mac's release coincides with a multimillion-dollar marketing campaign that presents it as a tool of personal liberation and social rebellion.

The Apple Macintosh personal computer, 1984

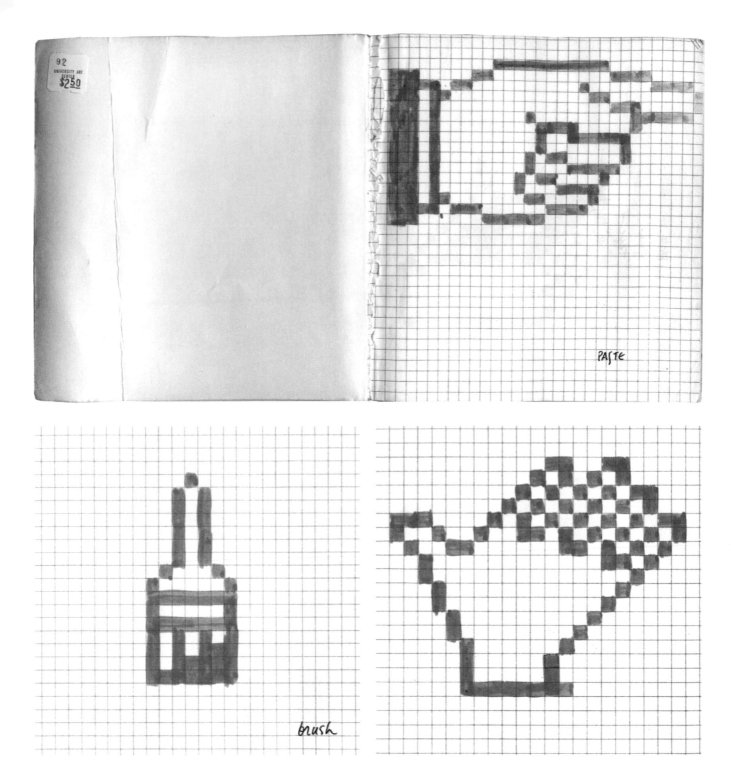

Above: Susan Kare, 'Sketches for a Graphic User Interface Icon', 1982
Opposite: Susan Kare, 'Happy Mac', 1982

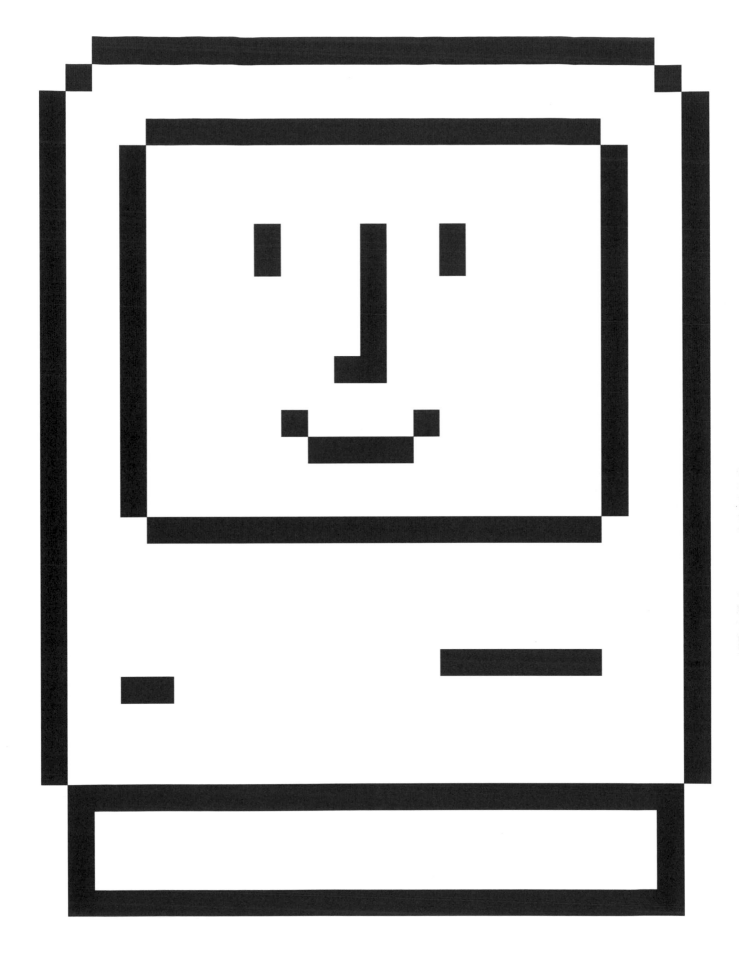

The Apple LaserWriter printer, 1985

One year after the Macintosh, Apple releases the LaserWriter. With its 12MHz CPU, 512KB of RAM and 1MB frame-buffer, it is a far more powerful machine than the Mac. Arguably, more influential too: combined with newly released publishing software Aldus PageMaker, the LaserWriter enables designers to preview and print page layouts complete with text and graphics – sparking the desktop-publishing revolution.

'Neomania', *Emigre* magazine, no. 24, 1992

The Berkeley-based magazine *Emigre* is one of the first to channel the power of the Mac. Working with a bitmap font tool, *Emigre* co-founder Zuzana Licko creates original typefaces for the magazine. Her fonts are designed as coarse bitmapped faces to accommodate low-resolution printer output. Together with her partner Rudy VanderLans, Licko uses the fonts to create layouts with varying type sizes, overlapping layers and text columns crashing into each other, all techniques that the Macintosh makes easier.

GREASING THE WHEELS OF CAPITALISM WITH STYLE AND TASTE *OR* THE "PROFESSIONALIZATION" OF AMERICAN GRAPHIC DESIGN

JUST SHOW ME THE MONEY

0. Mr. Keedy

THE ROLE that commerce has played in American graphic design, and how it has determined what is valued in design practice, is one of the most interesting and least discussed topics. Questions of an ethical nature seldom arise in design discourse because designers are used to deferring responsibility to their clients, who are ultimately accountable for what is produced. Designers are for the most part subordinate to the client, obedient to society, and patronizing to each other. The ethics of design are largely informed by a simplistic "politically correct" morality on one hand and a "bottom line" efficiency on the other, making for an easy value system for practice. It's a value system in which design is implicitly understood as a design service, in which it is the designer's responsibility to anticipate and satisfy the expectations of the client and audience.

THE PROBLEM with this arrangement is that the audience is for the most part a silent, indifferent, and undifferentiated entity, thus necessitating a surrogate (usually self-appointed) "expert" to become the spokesperson for the audience. This surrogate audience expert is usually the client, or worse, a marketing consultant hired by the client. This eliminates the possibility of the audience's desires contradicting the client's goals. On the other hand, the graphic designer as representative of the audience is just as likely to act with a fair dose of self interest. Neither the client armed with a team of marketing experts, nor the designer with the best of intentions, is a credible representative of the audience.

BUT WHAT IS THE ALTERNATIVE? The designer's and client's confidence that "we know what's best for you" is based on the fact that they do know and care a lot more about design than the audience does. The fact that the audience is often unwilling to concede this point is proof of the ignorance and contempt they have for any specialized knowledge and expertise in design. Perhaps that's why designers don't use the word "audience" very much anymore; now they call them "users." The term "user" is recognition of the fact that design and designers are supposed to be used by the users.

40

IN SPITE OF the general indifference most people have toward design, designers are hardly indifferent toward their users; in fact, they can't get enough of them. Who would have guessed that post-industrial capitalism would lead to so much selfless service to others' desires? But the "others," that designers are now so eager to please are not just some others, or most others; now we want to please all the others. Because nowadays, it often seems there is no problem in recording music, making a movie, or publishing a book without the guarantee of a huge audience, or maximum usability.

MOTIVATED BY GREED AND LAZINESS, this crowd-pleasing attitude has infected design. Now exposure has become more important than what's being exposed. The number of hits your web site gets, the number of fonts you sell, the number of design awards and magazine articles you can rack up, and how big your clients are, are what designers value most. Now bigger is better, particularly in regard to clients and users. Getting more users means getting younger ones. Just like music, film, clothing, and tobacco companies, now design companies are aiming lower for higher returns. It is without any sense of irony that designers now consider clients like Nike, Burton, and MTV the most desirable. AIGA design annuals that were once filled with great books, exhibition designs, and public signage systems, now look more like sporting goods catalogs for preteens.

JUST BECAUSE pop culture is ruled by adolescent taste, does that mean design culture has to follow the money? Since a designer's clients can never be too big, nor their audience too young, it would be logical to conclude that the really important design work of the future will be done for baby food and diapers, and the most desirable clients will be Gerber and Playskool.

IN DESIGN CIRCLES you often hear designers use the expression "selling out," but what does that mean in a practice in which the selling always precedes the production? And what exactly is being sold out? The designer's integrity and standards? What are those based on? Is design that doesn't attempt to make money somehow better than that which does? There has certainly never been a shortage of really crappy free design. The designer who believes that "selling out" is somehow easier than sticking to presumably higher principles has obviously never really sold out. Selling out is as much work and probably more aggravating than abiding by one's own self-fulfilling principles.

WHEN IT COMES TO the relationship between design and money, no one-to-one equation of value survives. Except maybe for the one that states: the bigger jerk the client is, the higher the charge. Or from the client's perspective: the bigger jerk the designer is, the higher the fee. But why would a client spend more money to work with a bigger jerk? It's like psychotherapy; if you don't pay for it, it doesn't work - no pain, no gain. "Just look at this fancy office, and all these employees and design awards, it's got to be worth the price. Right?"

1.!

2.

ECLECTICISM *AND* MODERNISM

41

IN THE EARLY DAYS, the commercial artist's aesthetic ideology was formed largely by the demands of the market place - whatever sold the best and was cost effective and expedient. That market-driven aesthetic was slightly tempered by the designer's personal experience that varied from print shops, sign painting, copy writing, and illustration. The aesthetic ideology of the commercial artist was a vernacular hodgepodge that had no preference for either high or low cultural value. Good or bad was only a matter of how well something was done. The only thing that was deemed unethical was to do amateurish and inept work for professional wages. Well crafted, or slickly

EMIGRE #70: THE LOOK BACK ISSUE | 242 | 1989
Text set in Base Monospace Wide Bold 7.5/11 point.
HEADLINES SET IN BASE MONOSPACE NARROW BOLD 10, 48 AND 200 POINT

Emigre magazine, no. 43, 1997

me, too.

Emigre magazine, no. 31, 1994

HHI

Emigre magazine, no. 11, 1989

Editor/Designer: RUDY VANDERLANS. Editorial consultant: ALICE POLESKY. Distribution, promotion and editorial assistance: ELIZABETH DUNN. Typeface design (this issue): BARRY DECK. Technical support: GERRY VILLAREAL. Emigre is published four times a year by Emigre Graphics. Copyright © 1991 Emigre Graphics. All rights reserved. No part of this publication may be reproduced without written permission from the contributors or Emigre Graphics. Emigre magazine is a trademark of Emigre Graphics. ISSN 1045- 3717. Send all correspondence to: Emigre, 48 Shattuck Square, №175, Berkeley, CA 94709 - 1140, USA. Phone (415) 845 9021. Fax (415) 644 0820. POSTMASTER PLEASE SEND ADDRESS CHANGES TO: EMIGRE, 48 SHATTUCK SQUARE, №175, BERKELEY, CA 94704 - 1140, USA. CIRCULATION 6,500. SUBSCRIPTIONS: $28 (four issues).

(Application to mail at 2nd class postage rates pending at Berkeley, CA.)

INTRRR ODUCT ION

Each time we bring one issue of *Emigre* to the printer, the idea for the next will have slowly started to surface, but never quite crystallizes until we're almost finished.

The idea for this issue started to come together after I was invited to do a three-day workshop at Cranbrook Academy of Art in Bloomfield Hills, Michigan.

I have always been impressed by the graphic design work produced there, mostly because of the students' high level of risk taking and experimentation. Regardless of the methodologies used I became far more interesting than what is expressed in the world, it is their sheer energy and sincere interest in graphic design as a creative discipline that I am attracted to. And although not everything they produce is of the same quality (some work I find downright ugly), the work usually manages to offer something new, raise questions, or make me laugh.

Over the past eight or nine issues, *Emigre* has often featured work by Cranbrook students and alumni alike. *Emigre* №10, published in 1989, was designed, written and produced entirely by the graduate design students.

Just recently a young undergraduate design student from a large university somewhere in the Midwest called me. He had picked up on my bias towards Cranbrook and asked me whether I thought that any of these "convention-and rule-breaking students at Cranbrook" were ever concerned about contributing in a "positive" way to our culture, instead of always breaking rules. He seemed both mad and frustrated. Mad, I believe, perhaps because he didn't understand this type of work, and frustrated (I found out later) because the school he attended left little room for such personal expression. After suggesting that he should address his question directly to the Cranbrook students, I did feel a need to inform him that, in my eyes, rule-breaking per se was not the goal. I told him that these graphic designers were trying to find their personal voice and were simply intrigued by the never-ending search for alternative ways to communicate visually and verbally. What better place to do this than in a graduate design program? I also mentioned that he should remember that the conventions and rules that exist within graphic design are not exactly carved in stone and that it is valid to question the necessity of these rules or at least wonder about how and why these rules were established in the first place. Graphic design is not like architecture where, for example, if you don't follow certain regulations, a building might collapse and kill people.

This doesn't mean that anything goes in graphic design. In the end, it is the designer's goal to communicate messages. But simple common sense is as good a rule to abide by as any. After my conversation with this student, I decided that this issue of *Emigre* should be devoted to

graphic designers who experiment – designers who are fascinated by the idea of what graphic design would be like if we didn't adhere to the existing rules. It would be an iconoclastic issue. "Why do we experiment?" would be the million dollar question.

However, during my three days at Cranbrook, another interesting notion came into the picture. Whenever the question arose of what the future of graphic design had in store, the students expressed a need to return to simpler, more direct ways of expression. This need had come partially as a reaction to ten years of very intense experimentation with complex typographic and pictorial structuring at Cranbrook beautifully elaborated upon and illustrated in the recently published book *Cranbrook Design: The New Discourse*. The current students, though, felt a need to take inventory and start with a clean slate. Such a reaction sounded familiar. After creating some of the most unconventional rule-breaking page layouts for the British *The Face* magazine, Neville Brody eventually returned to the very basics of graphic design or, as Keith Robertson writes in the following article, "the safe refuge of the International Style." When visiting Wolfgang Weingart last year, I was amazed when he showed me examples of his most recent work, they were simple typographic designs bearing little resemblance to his earlier layered typographic experiments. Dan Friedman, one of the initiators of American New Wave, is currently entirely satisfied with creating what some might consider non-design. The book *Artificial Nature*, which he designed in 1990, consists primarily of full bleed photographs with short captions set in Futura bold, set in horizontal black rectangles which are each centered in the middle of the page. Even Jan Tschichold, after setting the design world on fire with his manifesto *Die Neue Typographie* (what is considered a safe refuge now was then the most radical approach to graphic design imaginable), would later return to an even safer refuge: classical, center-axis typography. There are numerous other graphic designers I can think of who have traveled this path.

Is this a natural course that designers who experiment inevitably take? Does all experimentation in graphic design lead to the simplification of graphic design? Are graphic designers who concern themselves with complex solutions merely slow learners who try out the wildest schemes only to come to one conclusion, that less is more? Since we usually raise more questions with *Emigre* than we can answer, this seemed to be a topic right up our alley.

Rudy VanderLans

Emigre magazine, no. 19, 1991

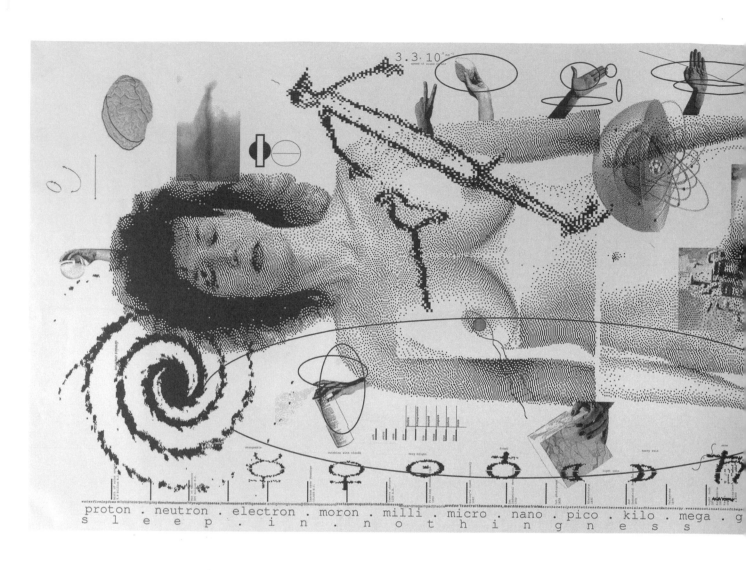

proton . neutron . electron . moron . milli . micro . nano . pico . kilo . mega . g

s l e e p . i n . n o t h i n g n e s s

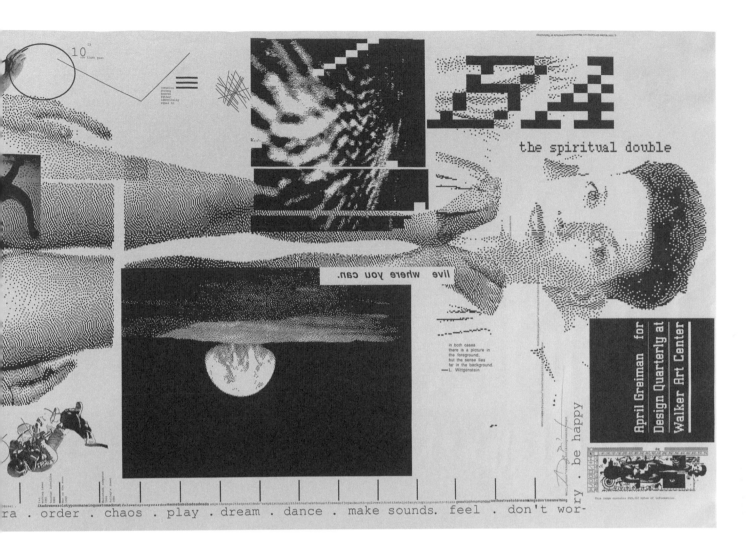

As Licko and VanderLans are assaulting the sacred tenets of magazine layout, LA designer April Greiman reinvents the format altogether. Her 1986 issue of *Design Quarterly* abandons the standard sixteen-spread sequence, reformatting it as a poster that folds out to almost three by six feet. She fills this tableau with an image of her digitized, naked body amid layers of interacting images and text. On the back, Greiman combines video images with comments and painstaking notations on her Mac-driven digital process.

April Greiman, 'Does it Make Sense?'
Design Quarterly, no. 133, 1986

JOIN WHO YOU WANT

Tools of Collaboration and Community

From the start, the freedom to live and work together has been essential to success and survival in California. Since the 1960s its designers have produced tools for expanding this freedom from the desert to the digital realm. They start with communes and concerts. By the 1980s, countercultural visions of a decentralized, systems-oriented society are powering the personal computing revolution. The early optimism of the communes shifts to the potential of virtual communities. The emergence of social media exponentially expands the size of online groups, but does little to counteract the atomization of society. To join who you want is also to ignore who you want.

TOOLS OF ONENESS

Design for Post-Industrial Communities

SIMON SADLER

How to feel at one – with oneself, with one's community, environment, technology, state, with people and things and ideas you don't know? Can that be designed, and, if so, then how – and where else than in California? The soap maker Emanuel Bronner, a refugee from the Holocaust, chose bottled soap as his unlikely medium. He proselytized his 'All-One' moral philosophy on the densely-printed labels for his 18-in-1 Pure Castile Soap, distributed from San Diego County.

> Replace half-true Socialist-fluoride poison & tax-slavery with full-truth, work-speech-press & profitsharing Socialaction! All-One! So, help build 4 billion Hannibal wind-power plants, charging 96 billion battery-banks, powering every car-factory-farm-home-monorail & pump, watering Babylon-roof-gardens ...

So reads a snippet from the soap's crazily long, stream-of-consciousness label. Still, it hit point after point of a long California counterculture: the dream of a bottom-up, entrepreneurial, caring and sharing, mystic, futuristic oneness of self and other. It's a paradigm, at once rather wonderful and rather scary. It might even be the hidden hand guiding, say, Elon Musk: at once a saviour of sustainable modernity and the potential supremo of a Tesla-SolarCity-SpaceX total system meshing clean cars with energy production and storage, with software and navigation, even with outer space – all as his loyal, community-forming customers secede from an older, big-oil paradigm.

Oneness courses through the spaces of Facebook – be that in its open-plan neo-warehouse campus, topped with a Bronner-esque roof garden, or in its colossal website that organizes global social relationships through virtual, constantly varying networks whose user experience can turn on a dime from tremendous intimacy to the ruthlessness of 'unfriending'. *Like!* is cosseting yet edgy: 'scouting a leading edge of technology which has an odd softness to it', as Stewart Brand, prophet of this oneness since the 1960s, explained of the hard-soft atmosphere of the communitarian tech frontier in 1972.[1]

California has a storied history of experimental, socialist and religious communities stretching back to the nineteenth century, which was rebooted (so to speak) by a long Californian counterculture.[2] From the 1940s onwards, there was a steady ascent of interest in 'human potential' assisted by retreats, seminars and meditation, in places such as Trabuco College, where college co-founder Aldous Huxley would write 'Lightly child, lightly. Learn to do everything lightly', capturing the state's ideal of unattached grace within its exceptional geography in his 1962 utopian novel, *Island*. The realization of the self and the other was pursued by the Beats; by the Esalen Institute of 1962; and, starting that same year, the San Francisco Zen Center and its offshoots (later frequented by Steve Jobs). Purposeful recreation, aided by drugs (especially cannabis, Benzedrine and LSD), music, parties and festivals – all tools, of a sort – entered the bloodstream of a counterculture that became more mass-organized and politicized

Page 156: Two women sit with groceries provided by the Black Panther Party's 'Free Food Program', Palo Alto, 1972
Above: Emanuel Bronner, Pure Castile Soap

with the 1964 Free Speech movement, anti-war agitation, support for civil rights and concern about ecology. Starting with the Haight-Ashbury crashpad scene, the counterculture's later phases radically extended the region's existing communitarian and communist traditions by building spaces for an alternative society. The contentious examples shown by the open-land and back-to-the-land movements of the mid-to-late 1960s – like the 1965 Hog Farm, Morningstar of 1966 (featured in *Time* the following year) and Wheelers Ranch of 1967 – gave patchy demonstrations of the possibility of 'bottom-up' community building.

Five years after the Free Speech protest at the University of California, Berkeley, peripheral university land awaiting redevelopment was occupied to become the anarchic and short-lived 1969 People's Park. If anything, the People's Park's chaotic culture and violent suppression (under then Governor Ronald Reagan) spurred a search for more enduring community organization, including the capture of the state. Following the 1975 election of a young, 'New Age' governor, Jerry Brown – to whom Stewart Brand was a consultant – one organizer of the People's Park, the Berkeley architecture professor Sim Van der Ryn, was appointed by Brown as State Architect. From this position he pursued a brief but vigorous programme of design promoting social and resource ecology for the state, including small-scale, localizing, energy-efficient 'appropriate technology'.[3] Even in government, Brand and Van der Ryn remained convinced that the state should be no more than an enabler of grassroots community design, like that of the Project One technological

commune of 'plumbers, computer freaks, architects and visionaries' in San Francisco that Stewart Brand reported on for *Rolling Stone* in 1972.

If we were to focus on just a single example of a Californian tool communitarian ethos, Project One would be a good choice. This applies right down to its name – One (like 'version 1.0', in coding parlance), as though the first of more, and One as in All-One (as in, 'Replace half-true Socialist-fluoride poison & tax-slavery ...'). 'No lazy hippies allowed' – so reported the politically progressive US magazine *Mother Jones* in its 1976 essay about life at Project One. 'No welfare types, no people who just want to stay stoned all the time ... Or wackies in any form, unless they were really into building a community and could prove it.'[4] From 1971 to 1980, Project One was a pioneer warehouse community, housing technologists and creative entrepreneurs, governed (barely) by consensus, consistent with a countercultural reaction against top-down hierarchy. It was initiated by architect and engineer Ralph Scott, a former student of Richard Buckminster Fuller, that popularizer of the geodesic dome (a countercultural icon) and a cult figure for a segment of the San Francisco Bay Area's hippie community coalescing around Stewart Brand's *Whole Earth Catalog*. Project One was like the *Catalog*'s vision of community become real – communitarians drifting through one another's workspaces in an interdisciplinary learning environment, complete with an Alternative High School. The *Whole Earth Catalog* strapline had promised 'Access to Tools', and tools like the computer were the key motif for the *Mother Jones*

People's Park, Berkeley, 1969

story on Project One – 'a whole tool-exploring community has formed in the building since One first opened its doors ... Tools were scammed, demystified and made free to anyone who wanted access to them.'[5] In addition to the computer, the 'building is a tool',[6] in which residents could also find tools for holography, sound-and-vision recording, photography and printing for community activism, ecological initiatives, women's rights and war resistance.

The greatest of Project One's tools was Resource One, a 'free-access computer center' operating a donated mainframe computer (some of its users graduated into the development of the personal computer).[7] Other countercultural communities at the time were based around what *Mother Jones* referred to as noble 'lower technologies' like baking and farming. (Following its foray into the rural hinterlands of the state, the hippie rediscovery of agriculture and food supply in California was to affect cuisine from winemaking to organic food and farmer's markets in the decades to come.) However, 'One's survival for six years has something to do with it being rooted in electronic-age technological skills'.[8] It was an *ur*-form of the start-up: in what has since become an idiom of contemporary architecture, Project One's cavernous warehouse space was broken up by its residents into plasterboard bays using tools for plumbing and wiring, and hammers, core-drillers and diamond guns. Touches of whimsy and break-out spaces (such as group baths) militated against the mid-century, white-collar 'cube farm'. 'The inside of One is painted like *A Clockwork Orange*

set,' *Mother Jones* reported, 'with endless orange, blue, crimson, rainbow-splashed hallways and stairwells ... There are flowing sculptured walls that weave in and out' (inspired by a former student of the ecological architect Paolo Soleri).[9] 'Project One is an internal village,' the article concluded, 'a high-technology pueblo.'[10]

A high-technology pueblo – not a bad description for the Facebook campus now nearing completion in Menlo Park under the direction of that quintessential Los Angeles architectural practice of (Frank) Gehry Partners. The Facebook campus's start-up atmosphere – realized through its large open-plan spaces, hanging cables and warehouse skylights – is being created *ex novo*, far from the repurposed warehouse space that accommodated Project One and initiatives like it four decades earlier. That's to say, Facebook is *designed*, and designed so well that the archetypal Californian outlook of the organic interrelation of place, community, technology, attitude and imagination *seems* natural, artless and unaffected – which in turn feeds the Californian self-image of *being* natural, artless and unaffected.

'Hack', announces the very paving of the Facebook piazza, to be read from the air, the word repeated around the campus (address: 1 Hacker Way). As Brand explained in his 1972 piece for *Rolling Stone*, 'Hackers are the ones who translate human demands into code that the machines can understand and act on ... Fanatics with a potent new toy.' 'Hacker' was also the term for a rapidly developing, self-identifying community, 'a term of derision and also the ultimate compliment'[11]

The 'Hack' courtyard at the Facebook Headquarters, Menlo Park, 2015

according to computer scientist Alan Kay in 1972, then at the epicentre of computer networking, the Xerox Research Center. Today, the 'hackers' of Facebook are perfecting the seemingly blank slate of a Facebook page and its iconic thumbs-up icon – endowing sharing, collaborating and fun itself with a distinct purposefulness. In this way, a once-utopian, and even religious, zeal still courses through California's now deeply strategic and profitable post-industrial products. Brand in 1971 described 'a mobile new-found elite, with its own apparat, language and character' living in 'outlaw country, where rules are not decree or routine so much as the starker demands of what's possible'.[12] Outlaw: a romantic, outsider identity was lodged within design for those who might transgress codes. In the early 1970s Sim van der Ryn would award his Berkeley architecture students, who sourced materials and built with them, with diplomas as 'Outlaw Builders'.

Initially, governmental hostility helped form an outlaw-community identity. This much was revealed during the Watergate hearings: Project One was under surveillance, to which its members responded by greeting a government spy team across the street with a camera crew, film lights and a videotape Portapak. But that wry wit, that active construction of community and identity, that live exploration of tools and collaborations are qualities of California post-industrial community which became perhaps reified, made more rote and less examined since. Outlaws are now as likely to 'disrupt' markets, conventions or disciplines as they are to brazenly break the law. Facebook's

business is to hew legal and electronic code to its collaborative model, so as to avoid the attention of regulation and law enforcement. Since the 1980s, perhaps the simple objective in the development of community and collaboration tools has been to make them more brilliant, commonplace and beautiful than ever before. Data sharing through UX, mobile phones, websites, server farms and personal computers has been integrated seamlessly; organic food can be enjoyed either at farmers' markets or as a TV dinner; and the radically, unstably ecological architecture of Sim van der Ryn and his students in the 1970s is now the epitome of sustainability.

Computing, Brand claimed in 1972, was 'a place' (note, the technologically bound social network as a *place*) 'where you can still be an artisan'.[13] Traditionally, an artisan wields tools of a skilled trade, pursuing high quality and restoring meaningful work, place, community and reality to post-industrial society – much as industrial-age activists in the nineteenth century attempted to reinstitute medieval affiliations through co-operative labour movements and the Arts and Crafts. That desire to restore a sense of connection to one's products and fellow-producers is now recognizable to people the world over (Project One quickly inspired an offshoot in Berlin, for instance), as sophisticated tools, culminating in 3D printers, are made available to those growing communities of 'Makers' organized by *Make* magazine – first published in San Francisco in 2005 and followed, in 2006, by the first Maker Faire. As the tools of community and collaboration become more commonplace, we might feel less like pioneers and more like products ourselves (generating monetarily valuable user data, for instance). The history of great tools in recent decades – the genre-making products of the Apple Corporation, including its Apple II (1977), Macintosh (1984) and its veritable 'electronic penknife', the iPhone (2007), entering its tenth anniversary – is as much a story of *perfecting* once-singular concepts as it is of creating new ones. Isolated in its quasi-natural environment of oaks, the Zen-like closed circle of Apple's new campus (by Norman Foster) lends an atmosphere of centered calm to a once-edgy culture.

Though it would remain seemingly forever 'the sixties for some segments of the subsequent tech industry, the shift from periphery to centre, from outlaw to mogul, was the price that California had to pay for being the first to prototype post-industrial civilization.[14] Nostalgia for outsider status is maybe nowhere better illustrated than at Burning Man, a festival which began with a 1986 summer-solstice bonfire ritual on San Francisco's Baker Beach and evolved into an annual instant city on the *playa* of Nevada's Black Rock Desert. At an event where typically more than half of the participants hold at least a bachelor's degree and where the most popular Burner career is in the computer and technology industries, Burning Man is in large part a bid by knowledge industry workers to restore frisson, imagination and camaraderie.[15] 'Once a homestead, America's largest urban commune is today rapidly evolving into a dormitory,'[16] Project One resident Charles Raisch was already complaining in his 1976 *Mother Jones* article. He noted that his One neighbours were starting to hire rather than collaborate or do things themselves. More troubling to him was that 'social unrest is at rest ... at One, after a remarkable revolutionary history, it's like the '50s all over again.'[17] Some residents of Project One were becoming painfully aware that physical proximity to other ethnicities, classes and cultures in San Francisco's South of Market neighbourhood did not necessarily mean integration. It's an inequity that techno-utopians hope will be ironed out over time (a classically liberal and neo-liberal belief), but California's startling post-industrial utopianism has never quite been truly utopian. 'You people are like children arguing about toys,' complained an African-American neighbour of Project One observing a meeting discussing whether to lock out the stereo of a resident in arrears. 'There is a struggle going on in this neighbourhood right now. People are organizing themselves just to get the essentials of life – a roof, a full belly, healthcare, a pair of shoes for their children, or their old man out of jail.'[18]

Even with this regrettable disconnect, the struggles of less-privileged Californians were contributing powerfully to the state's grassroots *élan*.[19] In Oakland (and eventually across the US), the community-building methods of the Black Panthers, like the 1969 Free Breakfast for School Children Program, simultaneously served the needs of a deprived population and made the cause of African-American disenfranchisement emblematic through a sensationally media-savvy campaign. Under César Chavez, the United Farm Workers, championing the principles of non-violence of Mahatma Gandhi and Martin Luther King, helped to make the notion of social justice part and parcel of the contemporary lexicon of community organization. More festive in intent, the California chop-shop and low-rider culture, serviced by a deep corridor of Southern Californian auto shops, tied together a Latin autopia. The Harley-Davidson motorbike, though built in the Midwest, became emblematic in the 1950s of white working-class masculinity as its devotees coalesced into gangs – most infamously, the California Hells Angels. In response to patriarchal cultures – the Angels at one extreme, California's sprawling suburbs at the other – the state's feminist communities coalesced around such interventions as the Womanhouse of 1972, adjacent to the California Institute of the Arts in Los Angeles.

Techno-utopianism – from the voluntary primitivism of the hippies to Silicon Valley's aggressive advocacy of immigration – actually identified with the precariousness of subjugation, population movement and economic cycles. These had formed California since the Gold Rush, the Great Migration and the Depression – empowering some and marginalizing others. As a flyer at Project One claimed, 'We were fooled in the same way the Okies were lured to California by the growers. Five jobs were promised when there was only one available. We were told that there would be an unlimited need for educated people – which was pure bullshit.'[20] So perhaps – *perhaps* – there is a recurrent 'all-one' in this version of California after all – as a space of struggle, potential, of appearance, of self-invention. California, the historian Carey McWilliams explained of the state's liberalism in 1949, is 'the great exception',[21] and the day after the infamously divisive 2016 US Presidential Election, California's legislative leaders issued a defiant, dual language, English/Spanish statement – a community-making tool of sorts – which claimed:

> California has long set an example for other states to follow. And California will defend its people and our progress. We are not going to allow one election to reverse generations of progress at the height of our historic diversity, scientific advancement, economic output and sense of global responsibility.[22]

The Ant Farm Media Van, Los Angeles, 1971

Built on natural capital (climate, forestry, gold, oil), business (agriculture, banking, media, high technology) and infrastructure (ports, railroads, water, social services, education and freeways – cemented by New Deal investments), California *as a state* could be claimed as *the* grand tool of collaboration and community. It's a tool that has been fought for: California has also been the illiberal domicile of Richard Nixon; of Ronald Reagan; of the 1978 taxpayers revolt of Proposition 13; and, latterly, of Silicon Valley's libertarianism, which assumes that society can be sustained merely by business, computing and charity. California has nearly been, in other words, a very different sort of place.[23] Its citizens have been profligate with its natural bounty – redwood forest clear-cut; rivers sedimented; wetland drained; land, groundwater and air contaminated. It has partaken heavily of that American community type – sprawl – which, whatever its guilty post-war charm, is unsustainable. It has, for all its entrepreneurial zeal, nurtured monopolies (like Southern Pacific and PG&E) and oligarchs (including, in fairness, Steve Jobs and Mark Zuckerberg) while shocking numbers of workers, notably in agriculture or based overseas but dependent on the state, struggle on the minimum wage and worse. It has had more than its share of racial tensions, from interwar house-purchasing covenants to inner-city inequalities of the sort that decimated LA's Watts in 1965 and South Central in 1992.

But then – *perhaps* – the bizarre contradictions of California are its unifier, laid upon this common 'plinth course',[24] in the words of the novelist Thomas Pynchon, of capital, infrastructure and narrative. In 1965 Charles Moore, the lead architect of the pioneering mid-1960s eco-community Sea Ranch, led bewildered readers from the northern end of the state – where his colleague Lawrence Halprin had diagrammed the project as an 'Ecoscore' of synchronized geology, species inhabitation, climate and human design – to the southern end of the state, where Moore wrote what would become the first serious consideration of Sea Ranch's nemesis: Disneyland. Both – in their striving for idealized authenticity – were wonderfully artificial American communities; Moore seemed to recognize this with his proto-post-modern eye. He further revelled in the contradiction of his essay's title, 'You Have to Pay for the Public Life', by tying the piece together through extolling the views from, and liberties afforded by, the private car – the very polluter restricted by the covenants signed by residents of Sea Ranch, whose existence had inspired the creation of the highways that are (Moore contended) the state's true public spaces.

As Moore traversed north to south at the wheel, he underscored the truism that the *automobile* was the make-or-break tool of the real-and-fictive California community. Even the hippies embraced the Volkswagen Microbus and Beetle, which was meanwhile amped-up by Bruce Meyers, who chopped and re-clad the Beetle with an open fibreglass body to make the dune buggy, sparking a worldwide community and competition between impersonators. That same year, 1964, provocateur Ken Kesey assembled his Merry Pranksters to drive coast to coast in a 1939 school bus to spread the message of dropping out, thus initiating another phase of the counterculture: 'Get On the Bus'. A Chevy was outfitted in 1971 by the absurdist Ant Farm art/architecture collective (formed, incongruously enough, at a Sea Ranch encounter devised by Halprin and Moore) as the Media Van, a nomadic television studio 'hacking' the media.

Massive investments in mass transit are today taking hold in California – downtown rail is transforming an urban corridor of Los Angeles, and a proposed high-speed rail system could yet link the northern and southern ends of the state; California's city streets are being 'hacked' by 'parklet' public space created from parking lanes and parking spaces, with an annual meter-feeding Parking Day, initiated in San Francisco in 2005, now spread worldwide. But despite a choking smog completely unmanaged until the early 1960s, when California demanded the first anti-smog controls on cars, the sprawl of LA became a global paradigm of mobile, individualist, market freedoms. Communities, sociologist Melvin Webber argued from California in 1964, are bound not by civic society or physical proximity but by jobs, interests, cars and the telephone[25] – today, by cellular and wireless technology. In 2013 Google's buses, prowling San Francisco in search of employees (who clock on to work upon entry) provided a flashpoint for activists protesting against the private use of public streets and bus stands by a tech elite escalating the costs of real estate. (As a momentary refuge from tech-driven rent increases in San Francisco, disused commercial space across the water in Oakland has attracted live/work experiments, gaining tragic attention in the wake of the December 2016 fire that swept through the Ghost Ship warehouse, taking thirty-six lives.)

The tools of Californian community, it seems, are those that accelerate self-invention and the contingencies of California's geography, infrastructure and economy. At the beginning of the 1970s, the British historian of architecture and design, Reyner Banham, influentially described Los Angeles as an 'ecology'.[26] Much as Bronner's soapy credo would have it: the Californian all-one is a sunny environment of sought personal freedom, mediated peer-to-peer, vexed by the knowledge that all this is not *really* the all-one after all.

1 • S Brand, 'Spacewar: Fanatic Life and Symbolic Death among the Computer Bums', *Rolling Stone* (7 December 1972), <wheels.org/spacewar/stone/rolling_stone.html>

2 • The key historian of US communitarianism is Timothy Miller: see, for instance, 'California Communes: A Venerable Tradition', in I Boal, J Stone, M Watts and C Winslow (eds.), *West of Eden: Communes and Utopia in Northern California* (Oakland, 2012), 3–12.

3 • See S Sadler, 'The Bateson Building, Sacramento, California, 1977–81, and the Design of a New Age State', *Journal of the Society of Architectural Historians*, vol. 75, no. 4 (December 2016), 469–89.

4 • C Raisch, 'Pueblo in the City', *Mother Jones* (May 1976), 29–34, 29.

5 • *Ibid.*, 30–1.

6 • *Ibid.*, 34.

7 • *Ibid.*, 32.

8 • *Ibid.*, 32.

9 • *Ibid.*, 31.

10 • *Ibid.*, 29.

11 • Brand, 'Spacewar'.

12 • *Ibid.*

13 • *Ibid.*

14 • On the architectural conservatism of Silicon Valley, see A Arieff, 'Facebook Plays it Safe', *New York Times* (31 August 2012), <opinionator.blogs.nytimes.com/2012/08/31/facebook-plays-it-safe/?_r=2>

15 • See X Clark, 'Burning Man census reveals surprising demographics at the desert festival' (14 October 2012), <archive.peninsulapress.com/2012/10/14/burning-man-census-reveals-surprising-demographics-at-the-desert-festival/#ed>. See, too, J Harkinson, 'Silicon Valley Firms Are even Whiter and more Male than You Thought', *Mother Jones* (29 May 2014), <motherjones.com/media/2014/05/google-diversity-labor-gender-race-gap-workers-silicon-valley>

16 • Raisch, 'Pueblo in the City', 34.

17 • *Ibid.*

18 • *Ibid.*

19 • For a sense of Californian creative diversity, see, for instance, S Barron, S Bernstein and I Susan Fort (eds.), *Reading California: Art, Image, and Identity* (Berkeley, 2000); and *Made in California: Art, Image, and Identity, 1900–2000* (Berkeley, 2000).

20 • Raisch, 'Pueblo in the City', 32.

21 • See C McWilliams, *California, The Great Exception* (Berkeley, 1949).

22 • Joint Statement from California Legislative Leaders on Result of Presidential Election (9 November 2016), <sd24.senate.ca.gov/news/2016-11-09-joint-statement-california-legislative-leaders-result-presidential-election>

23 • For this analysis, I am indebted to the work of UC Berkeley geographer Richard Walker. See, for instance, R Walker and A Schafran, 'The Strange Case of the Bay Area', *Environment and Planning A*, vol. 47 (2015), 10–29.

24 • T Pynchon, *The Crying of Lot 49* (1965) (reprinted: New York, 2006), 13.

25 • See M Webber, 'The Urban Place and the Non-Place Urban Realm', in M Webber et al. (eds.), *Explorations into Urban Structure* (Philadelphia, 1964).

26 • See Reyner Banham, *Los Angeles: The Architecture of Four Ecologies* (Harmondsworth, 1973).

Construction of an elliptical dome at the Pacific High School, a free-form, live-in learning community, 1970

Bob Allen and Jon Smith, Pacific High School, 1970

Following the Summer of Love in 1967, thousands of hippies leave San Francisco as part of the largest wave of communalization in American history.

For the participants, communalization is the start of what could be a new nation, a reinvented America of small, egalitarian communities linked to one another by a network of shared beliefs. Depicted in the *The Teacher was the Sea: The Story of the Pacific High School* and deployed on hippy communes across California, the geodesic dome is the emblem of a new, non-hierarchical society.

Top Left: Teachers and students of Pacific High School, Menlo Park, 1970
Top Right: Construction of an elliptical dome at the Pacific High School, 1970
Bottom Left: Lloyd Kahn, teacher at the Pacific High School, 1970
Bottom Right: Students of Pacific High School, 1970

Stanley Mouse, 'The Human Be-In' poster on the cover of the *City of San Francisco Oracle*, vol. 1, no. 5, 1967

Bruce Reifel, 'Gay-In' poster, 1970

California's hippy counterculture bursts into national consciousness via a gathering in Golden Gate Park. Announced on the cover of the January 1967 issue of the *San Francisco Oracle*, organizers urge attendees to bring flowers, families, incense and animals to 'a gathering of the tribes for a Human Be-In'.

Three years later, the Los Angeles chapter of the activist group Gay Liberation Front holds a 'gay-in' in Griffith Park as a means of increasing the visibility of the city's gay and lesbian community and mobilizing the next generation of gay rights activists.

Map of the Merry Pranksters' road trip around North America, as recounted in *The Electric Kool-Aid Acid Test,* 1968

California's psychedelic culture spreads across North America via a coast-to-coast-and-back road trip conducted by the author Ken Kesey and a group of friends and followers known as the Merry Pranksters. The literal and philosophical engine is Furthur [sic.], a painted school bus from which the Pranksters spread the gospel of hippy counterculture by organizing happenings and handing out LSD.

Merry Pranksters leader Ken Kesey atop the Furthur [sic.] bus, 1966

Neal Cassady and psychedelic research pioneer Timothy Leary on the Furthur [sic.] bus, 1964

County Sheriff questioning Satan's Slave motorcycle club bikers during a ride from San Bernardino to Bakersfield, 1965

California's hippy counterculture exists uneasily with the state's many motorcycle clubs. In contrast to the Day-Glo decorations of the hippies, outlaw motorcycle clubs apply 'colors' in the form of patches that identify membership, rank, territorial location and in some cases political views.

Satan's Slaves motorcycle club vest, 2012

Sheila Levrant de Bretteville, 'Eyebolt' necklace, 1972

California's female designers devise symbols of their own. For the Women in Design conference, Sheila de Bretteville designs a poster and an entry pass. Both emphasize the eyebolt, a common piece of hardware that de Bretteville repurposes to evoke the biological symbol of women.

Sheila Levrant de Bretteville, poster for the 'Women in Design' conference, 1974

Lead engineer William English tests the first mouse demo on the oN-Line System (NLS), 1968

The notion of virtual community emerges in concert with the countercultures of the 1960s, largely through the efforts of Douglas Englebart.

Between 1966 and 1968 Englebart and colleagues at the Stanford Research Institute develop a collaborative computing environment known as the oN-Line System, or NLS. The NLS introduces many of the defining elements of personal computing, including the mouse and QWERTY keyboard. More importantly, the system offers its users the ability to collaborate on a document simultaneously from multiple sites, to connect bits of text via hyperlinks, and to video conference.

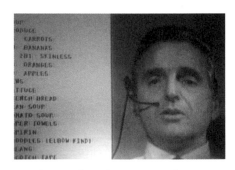

Douglas Engelbart demonstrates the NLS, 1968

Gordon French speaks at a Homebrew Computer Club meeting, Menlo Park, 1978

Throughout the 1970s a new generation of computer enthusiasts builds on Englebart's innovations. They meet in an informal hobbyist group, the Homebrew Computer Club, to trade parts, circuits and information on the DIY construction of computing devices. Several high-profile hackers and computer entrepreneurs emerge from the group, including Apple's Steve Wozniak and Steve Jobs.

I am a self-employed productivity consultant. I live out in the country overlooking the ocean near Bodega Bay. The phone, fax, and e-mail let me work here, and still be in the business community.

***

I reside in Seoul Korea where I practice public relations for the U.S. government.

***

I am a physiciam, specializing in women's health, including contraception, abortion, and estrogen replacement therapy after menopause. I am the medical director of an abortion clinic. I was a member of the Mid-Peninsula Free University in the 70's and organized concerta, including the Dead, Big Brother, Quicksilver, Jefferson Airplane, etc. I am interested in philosophical/ethical issues surrounding the beginning of life and the end of life and the functional value of rituals and traditions.

***

I am a 19 year old college student struggling to find myself. I enjoy sitting in a field of dandelions with no socks. I spend too much time playing on my computer. I am an advertising/business major so I will be here for five or more years. I am trying to find the meaning of life ... helpful hints are appreciated. I with that penguins could have wings that worked (Breathed), solutions are being contemplated ...

***

I am a student from Prague, Czechoslovakia, studying in San Francisco's Center for Electronic Art computer graphic and design programs.

***

Librarian for USDA, sysop of "ALF" bbs

***

I am a lawyer, working as a law clerk to 3 state judges in Duluth. I am 31 and single. I graduated from the Naval Academy in 1982, and the University of Minnesota Law School in 1990. I opposed the Gulf War, and I was Paul Wellstone's deputy campaign director in the 8th Congressional District. I like sailing and long hikes in the woods and the shore. My other interests include law and Italy. My biggest issues today are single payer universal health care and proportional representation.

***

I'm interested in land-use planning (I'm helping to put together the Sacramento County General Plan), and in Management of Information Systems (I'm writing an article about this, and am interested in a career in it). I'm a real estate broker and developer now, with several years experience using and reviewing software for IBM-compatibles.

***

I am a born-again phreak, at age 33. My modem is my life! OK, the weightlifting, the fast care, they are all fun, but the modem is the biggie! As a matter of fact, I met my husband on a bbs! But, I realize that I have only tapped the surface of what my little Hayes can do, and I want to learn it all!

***

I am a self-employed systems and software consultant, primarily on large military command-and-control systems. My newest interests are in neural networks and fuzzy logic, with parallel processing as an enabling technology. I am usually interested in discussing new technologies and new applications of technology, along with the societal implications, with almost anybody, anywhere, anytime.

***

Music Store owner, Secretary of Ecological Economics of Alaska.

***

Captain, US Army

***

I am a Japanese writer who are very much interested in ecology and the electronic democracy. I am going to spend two years with studying (joining?) ecological movement and sharing network as a tool for making the new world here in Berkeley.

WELL member autobiographies, collected by Howard Rheingold, 1991–2

In 1985 the bible of the back-to-the-land movement becomes one of the world's first computer networks, as the creators of the *Whole Earth Catalog* launch the Whole Earth 'Lectronic Link (or WELL).

The proto-social network brings together former counter-culturalists, hackers and journalists, some of whom will eventually go on to make *Wired* magazine. Decades later, *Wired* becomes the connective tissue of a community of seemingly disconnected demographics.

THE WIRED INSIDERS

WIRED

A Community Powered by Social Capital

IT GIRL
This wired up woman can come to your rescue with the techie tool kit she's toting in her Chrome bag. She always knows which piece of hardware will make your life easier.

CULTURAZZI
Don't go head-to-head in a game of trivia with WIRED's resident culture vulture, who'll always out-Simpsons quote you and knows the secrets behind Inception's soundtrack.

GASTRONAUT
Kiss your average sunny-side ups goodbye. This mad scientist meets foodie will cryo gun your cocktails, sous vide your chops, and explain the tech behind biodynamic wine.

DIGITAL GENTLEMAN
This well-appointed gentleman has a penchant for pretty tech. Expect to see him relaxing in his Herman Miller, with a nice tumbler of whiskey, and perusing WIRED on his leather-encased iPad.

ADVENTURE CAPITALIST
This fan of extremes can swim the Polar Bear Challenge and has an arsenal of tech tools that'll tell you how many calories he burned and how much REM sleep he'll need to recover.

SMARTER UPSTARTER
He might have long hours, but check out the Kinect in his cube, or catch him at SXSW, and you'll see that this smart, savvy, and ambitious member of the Valley Pack has perfected the science of 'bleisure.'

MAKER
Hackers, modders, fabbers, tweakers. These 'passionate amateurs' are building their own blimps, reducing their footprint, and customizing their cribs sans the help of so-called professionals.

CHIEF DISRUPTOR
This boardroom executive didn't just write the book on the future, he made it happen. He brings ideas to life and impacts the very way we live. Everyone knows his name in the Valley, in the Capital, and at Davos.

Excerpt of the *Wired* magazine media kit, 2015

Video stills from the third Burning Man festival, 1988

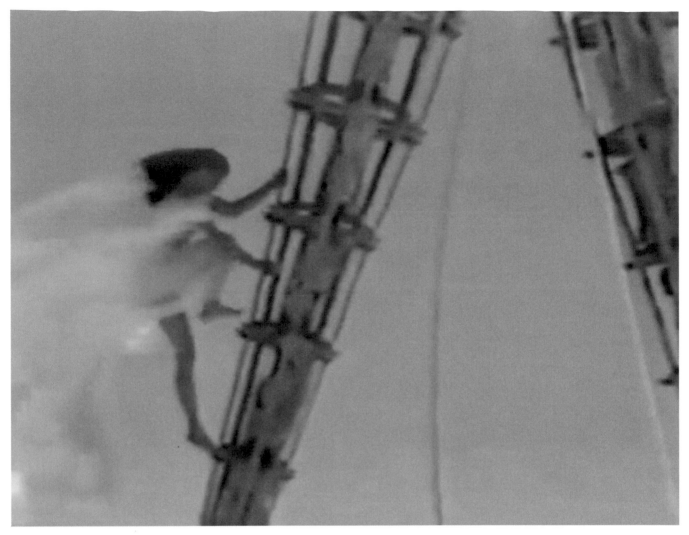

Above: A performer scales the wooden leg of the 'Burning Man' effigy, 1991
Following Spread: The Burning Man festival, aerial view, 2014

Tech enthusiasts do not only come together online, they also commune with fire.

The annual experiment in conditional community known as Burning Man begins with a handful of friends lighting a bonfire on Baker Beach in San Francisco. It eventually outgrows its place of birth, expanding into the Nevada desert and attracting revellers from around the world.

Los Angeles hosts the Olympics in 1984. Challenged to achieve maximum impact with minimum means, the environmental designer Deborah Sussman devises a graphic kit of parts capable of tying together disparate venues and creating the illusion of coherence for the TV audience.

The scheme embodies the multicultural melting pot of California, using a palette of 'Pacific Rim' colours to make a vibrant identity that Sussman names 'Festive Federalism'.

This Spread: Snapshots of the 1984 Olympic games in Los Angeles
Following Spread: Sussman-Prezja, Olympic graphic identity guidelines, 1984

A Preview of the

DESIGN

for the 1984 Olympic Games

How the Los Angeles Olympic Organizing Committee will transform the city with an exciting program of festive elements.

Every perception of the Games of the XXIII Olympiad will be a complex array of temporal elements juxtaposed against the highly varied background of Los Angeles and its environs. The LAOOC has developed a very strong thematic philosophy for the creation of the Olympic environment that will overlay the city during the Games. An energetic montage of color and form will appear on everything from tents to tickets.

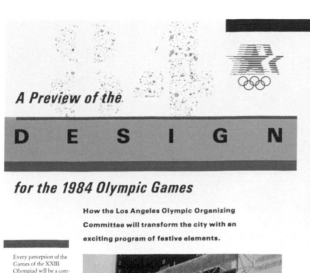

These brightly painted cylindrical columns will be sprinkled throughout the competition sites. Bands of brilliant color combined in different ways produce their playful quality.

These tents, whose prismatic shapes are color coded as to function, are intermixed with the other design elements to

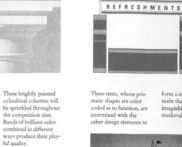

"... the city will be transformed overnight, a invasion of butterflies has descended upon it"

form a mode ment that rec imageable qua medieval jou

Painted scaffold assemblies will be enriched with color and graphics to form monumental gateways, towers and walls.

"It's not just how they're

HOW TO

1984 Olympic Games: Environmental design and color developed for the LAOOC by Sussman/Prejza & Co. in collaboration with The Jerde Partnership

A Guide to the

COLOR

The key color for the 1984 Olympic Games is a brilliant "hot" magenta. This color, together with bright vermilion, clean aqua, rich chrome yellow and vivid green represent the Southern California spirit. The lighter "mediterranean" colors are used occasionally in large backgrounds. White is used a great deal as a dignified link throughout the environment. Red, white and blue is only used on the rare occasion when it is appropriate to emphasize nationalism instead of the traditional Olympic internationalism.

For color specifications, contact LAOOC Design Department at 305-8814.

1 Magenta

Vermilion **Aqua** **Chrome Yellow**

Info Yellow **Green** **Lavender** **Light Blue**

Violet **Blue** **Pink**

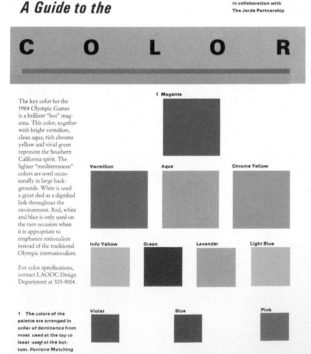

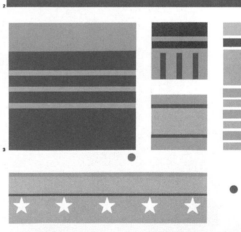

$ ¥ fr £

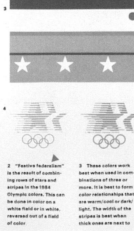

1 The colors of the palette are arranged in order of dominance from most used at the top to least used at the bottom. Pantone Matching System (PMS) numbers are listed to help in specifying these colors.

"... the absence of the grandiose and the festivity of color."

2 "Festive federalism" is the result of combining rows of stars and stripes in the 1984 Olympic colors. This can be done in color on a white field or in white, reversed out of a field of color

3 These colors work best when used in combinations of three or more. It is best to form color relationships that are warm/cool or dark/light. The width of the stripes is best when thick ones are next to

thin ones and when the arrangement is put on a large field of color or a white field.

4 The Star-in-Motion may appear in any of the 1984 Olympic colors or white on a strong color in addition to the red, white and blue scheme.

5 When enlarged, the Star-in-Motion creates a strong graphic pattern. These uses include the copyright and trademark designations. Original Star-in-Motion design by Robert Miles Runyan & Assoc.

6 When us sports picto symbol sign appear in wh magenta fie magenta pic also be com an additiona color such a

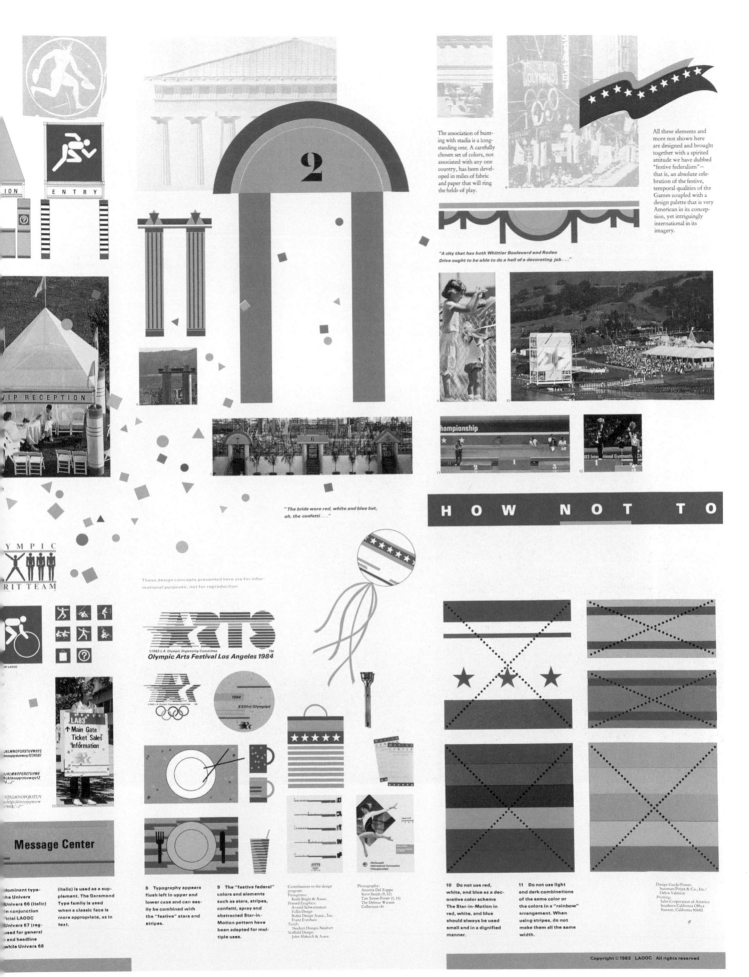

The association of bunting with stadia is a long-standing one. A carefully chosen set of colors, not associated with any one country, has been developed in miles of fabric and paper that will ring the fields of play.

All these elements and more not shown here are designed and brought together with a spirited attitude we have dubbed "festive federalism"— that is, an absolute celebration of the festive, temporal qualities of the Games coupled with a design palette that is very American in its conception, yet intriguingly international in its imagery.

"A city that has both Whittier Boulevard and Rodeo Drive ought to be able to do a hell of a decorating job . . ."

"The bride wore red, white and blue but, oh, the confetti . . ."

HOW NOT TO

These design concepts presented here are for informational purposes, not for reproduction.

Olympic Arts Festival Los Angeles 1984

1984
XXIIIrd Olympiad

ENTRY

Message Center

↑ Main Gate
Ticket Sales
Information

8 Typography appears flush left in upper and lower case and can easily be combined with the "festive" stars and stripes.

9 The "festive federal" colors and elements such as stars, stripes, confetti, spray and abstracted Star-in-Motion pattern have been adapted for multiple uses.

dominant type-
the Univers
Univers 66 (italic)
in conjunction
icial LAOOC
Univers 67 (reg-
sed for general
and headline
while Univers 68

(italic) is used as a supplement. The Garamond
Type family is used
when a classic face is
more appropriate, as in
text.

Contributions to the design program:
Pictograms:
Keith Bright & Assoc.
Printed Graphics:
Arnold Schwartzman
Follis Design
Robot Design Assoc., Inc.
Franz Eemhuis
Torch:
Neubart Donges Neubart
Scaffold Design:
John Aleksich & Assoc.

Photography:
Annette Del Zoppo
Steve Smith (9, 10)
Tim Street-Porter (1, 11)
The Delmar Watson
Collection (8)

10 Do not use red, white, and blue as a decorative color scheme The Star-in-Motion in red, white, and blue should always be used small and in a dignified manner.

11 Do not use light and dark combinations of the same color or the colors in a "rainbow" arrangement. When using stripes, do not make them all the same width.

Design Guide/Poster:
Sussman/Prejza & Co., Inc.
Debra Valencia
Printing:
Sales Corporation of America
Southern California Office
Stanton, California 90680

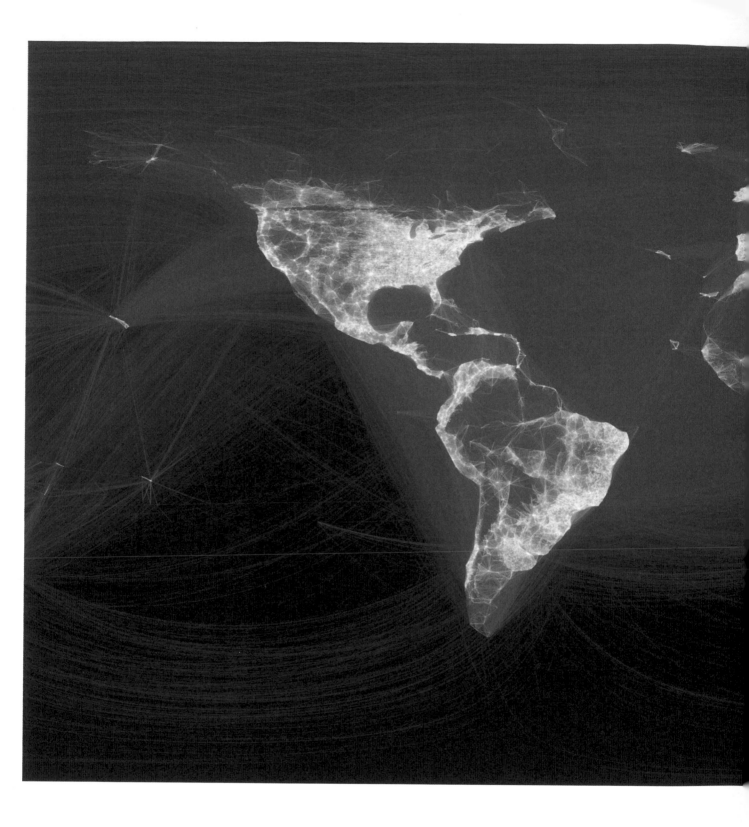

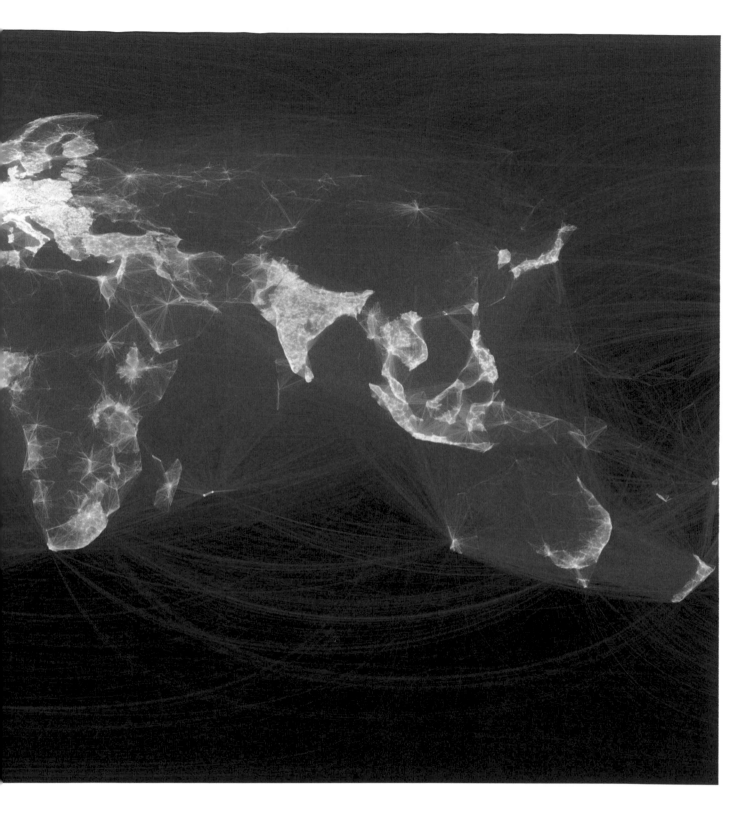

A map created by Facebook suggests a new way to see the world. Each line connects cities with pairs of Facebook friends. The brighter the line, the more friends between those cities. The result is a new kind of projection for the social network age, with political borders replaced by human relationships.

Paul Butler, Visualization of pairs of Facebook friends, 2010–15

As more and more interactions occur on screen, social media develop substitutes for the nonverbal cues that make up the majority of offline communication. The Facebook 'Like' provides a way to express support without going into specifics.

'Likes' form a whole economy of approval, used to boost one's self-esteem and business.

Facebook, 'Like' icon, 2016

The Echo, Amazon's voice-controlled intelligent personal assistant, points to a future in which we commune with our computers with no typing at all.

This the most significant development in computing since the smartphone.

The Amazon Echo smart speaker, 2016

Scott Boms, 'Why Haven't We Seen the Whole World Connected Yet?', 2016

The posters produced by Facebook's Analog Research Lab embody the 'fail fast' ethos of Silicon Valley. The rush to 'ship' a product is driven by a belief that our collective intelligence – the hive mind – will improve it more efficiently than any old fashioned internal review.

DONE IS BETTER THAN PERFECT

POSTER BROUGHT TO YOU BY YOUR FRIENDS AT THE FACEBOOK ANALOG RESEARCH LABORATORY

Ben Barry, 'Done Is Better than Perfect', 2011

We shape our tools and they in turn shape us.

Marshall McLuhan

Tim Belonax, 'We Shape Our Tools', 2014

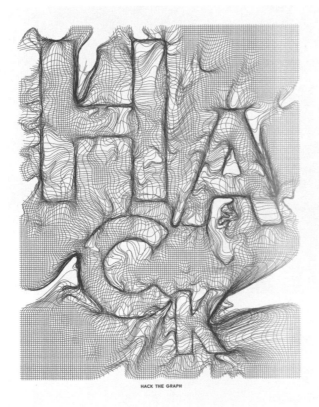

HACK THE GRAPH

Tim Belonax, 'Hack', 2014

MOVE FAST AND BREAK THINGS

POSTER BROUGHT TO YOU BY YOUR FRIENDS AT THE FACEBOOK ANALOG RESEARCH LABORATORY

Ben Barry, 'Move Fast and Break Things', 2011

The campuses of California's tech giants embody their corporate philosophies.

Facebook's is communitarian, with the largest open-plan office in the world; Apple's is insular, like a perfect, hermetic product; Google's is utopian, a land of work-play in a 1960s style high-tech tent.

Usually embedded in Edenic suburbs, far removed from the lively mess of the city, the tech campus represents the latest step in the evolution of the communalist vision espoused by California's hippies five decades ago.

Above: Foster + Partners rendering, Apple Park, Cupertino, completed 2017
Pages 226–7: Google's data centre in Council Bluffs, Iowa, 2012

INTERVIEWS

Fred Turner
Kevin Kelly
Matías Duarte
April Greiman
David Kelley
Yves Béhar

FRED TURNER

Interview by Justin McGuirk

- Turning cars into geodesic domes
- The military origins of Silicon Valley
- How utopia and self-interest merged

Your book *From Counterculture to Cyberculture* was one of the inspirations behind our approach to contemporary Californian design. Our curatorial device was the notion that California specializes in tools of personal liberation – the idea that design puts tools in your hand that enable you to be more self-sufficient or fulfilled. This idea arguably originates in the counterculture, so can you talk about the idea of the tool in that moment?

To understand what a tool was for the counterculture, we have to understand that there were in fact two countercultures. In the 1960s we have the New Left, forming parties like Students for Democratic Society and marching against the [Vietnam] war. But there was another counterculture, which I've called the New Communalists, who wanted to step away from politics entirely. They wanted to build new communities focused on the raising of consciousness and on personal liberation. Those communities were entirely engaged with technology. Not big technology; they were against large weapon systems, they were against mass industrial technology, but they were all in favour of taking devices that had been developed by those worlds and repurposing them into tools for everyday living. Between '66 and '73, hundreds of thousands of people moved to communes, and they hoped when they got there to find things like LSD, stereos, the automobile, things that had been provided by industrial America and to turn them into tools for changing their minds, for building new kinds of community around shared consciousness.

It's important, for the purposes of our argument, that this hippie movement was co-opting or repurposing the tools of the military-industrial complex.

We often think of the counterculture as something that turned away from black and white, Cold War, hierarchical America. On the contrary, they actually embraced key parts of it. One figure they embraced was Buckminster Fuller. Buckminster Fuller was a technocrat. He was an architect, a kind of peripatetic designer, and he had an idea that was born around 1941 which was 'comprehensive design'. He thought that what we should do was take things that were made by large-scale industries, and valve them – he used the word 'valve'. Bring them down to the scale of everyday life, and use them as tools for personal transformation. His theory was that the world had enough in the way of resources. They were just badly distributed. And so the job of the comprehensive designer was to take resources and redistribute them into everyday life. When they did that, everyday life would be genuinely political in a way that a world ruled by industry never could be. Commune folks took this up in spades. They went to Drop City in 1965, chopped the roofs off cars and tacked them together into geodesic domes. Geodesic domes were meant to be tools valved from the products of mainstream America and transformed into technologies within which you could become kind of a whole person, that a 'square house' would never let you be.

And how do these rather humble creations become a way of taking on the system?

The countercultural idea of the tool was in many ways a rebellion against the idea of the system. In the 1940s and 1950s, people like Norbert Wiener reimagined the world as an information system, and that was the managerial ethos of the time. People who ran large corporations, or universities, were all about creating the systems within which people were meant to be free individuals, and to which individuals were meant to adjust themselves. Therapy centres at the time were even called 'Adjustment Centres'. The trouble with that was that systems were very far from individual life. And one of the things the counterculture tried to do was develop small technologies that would let a person negotiate a new relationship to the system. LSD is a classic example of this. You take LSD, you are taking an industrial product, literally valving industrial technology into your body, as Buckminster Fuller said you should. Then, once it's in your body, through your senses, it lets you see the hidden, organic connectedness of all things, which is a strange imitation of exactly what Norbert Wiener said the world should be in his 'Cybernetics'. And the irony here is that Norbert Wiener's 'Cybernetics' inspires both a kind of psychedelic vision, and the managerial vision by which people manage firms like General Motors. This idea that 'the world's a system and I need to figure out how to be in it' is an idea that animates mainstream America *and* countercultural America. The tool is what lets you take your body and be in control of your relationship to the system. That's why the very first section of the *Whole Earth Catalog* is called 'Whole Systems'.

The hippies legitimated the rise of computing. In the 1960s and early 1970s, computers were the emblem of the Cold War American state and the people who worked on them had no cultural legitimacy.

You once told me that design is politics. You said that we used to do politics through government, but that design is the everyday politics of a technology-enabled world.

One of the things about Cold War America was that it was a time when there was a great turning away from traditional politics, from the top down, hierarchical politics that brought us the Vietnam War. What's going to come in their place? Well, in a lot of ways design becomes politics. It's what works when the state doesn't. When you have a tool-enabled world, you want to use your tools to design your life, to be more liberated. This is particularly true on communes, where coming together and trying to form communities of consciousness is a process by which people try to actually let go of hierarchical politics, let go of the state. What do you put in there instead? What's your mechanism for control? Well, you start designing. You design clothes, gatherings, houses, you try to make environments which will themselves become tools to enhance your personal and collective liberation.

This DIY ethic is crucial to the way military and corporate technology finds its way into the mainstream, isn't it? Hippies and hobbyists appropriate these technologies, but they're not necessarily anti-business.

Again, it's funny: we think of the counterculture as something that rebelled against mainstream America, and the methodology promoted by companies such as Apple suggests that Steve Jobs and Steve Wozniak were somehow rebels, gathered together in a kind of hippy enclave, sneaking out technologies of the mainstream military-industrial complex and putting them to work in these new, empowering technologies. Not quite true. Silicon Valley was itself an area imbued with military and industrial technology from the 1920s on. What the hippies did was they legitimated the rise of computing. In the 1960s and early 1970s, computers were the emblem of the Cold War American state, and the people who worked on them had no cultural legitimacy.

Fast-forward now to the early 1980s. The counterculture has collapsed, Ronald Reagan is president, and Stewart Brand and Ken Kesey are wondering what happened. They thought they were going to change the world. In the meantime, those military firms have spawned small, desktop computers, and Stewart Brand gathers the people making those at the first Hackers Conference in 1984 in San Francisco for a long weekend. And when they come together, the computer folks are first most interested in talking about new computer models. But, very quickly, they start talking to the counterculturalists who are there, left-over folks from the *Whole Earth Catalog* world, and they begin to imagine themselves as agents of countercultural change. This is one of those key moments when new modes of commercial entrepreneurship become entangled with old modes of countercultural being.

Is it fair to say that by the 1990s a new generation of tech entrepreneurs think they can use technology to change the world?

The history of California computing is a constant entanglement of commercial and utopian aims. In the counterculture, business was the way to achieve utopia. The state was bankrupt, government didn't work: business was the way to go. By the late 1990s in the Bay Area, we have the Internet, and a new generation of programmers and system builders, some from the Bay Area like the folks who founded Google and went to school at Stanford, and others from Harvard, like Mark Zuckerberg, but who came quickly to the Valley. And when they arrive, they walk into a world in which the pursuit of utopia by commercial means is a given. Both impulses are seen as true and authentic. When Google says 'Don't be evil', they really mean 'Do the right thing. Pursue utopian goals.' But if you probe a little bit, you say 'well, what's good?' and they say 'providing information is good'. 'Who provides information?' 'Well, Google provides information.' And suddenly you're back in that loop. What's good for Google is good for the world. But I think both sides of this are quite authentic. I think people genuinely see the pursuit of online information and community, and the pursuit of profit, as two sides of the same coin. Of course, this is a deeply American, deeply Protestant, idea.

We've been talking about personal liberation and breaking free of a technocratic world, but what is the nature of this 'liberation'?

We often imagine that liberation is a condition of breaking away from a larger world. On one level that's true, but the kind of personal liberation that people are pursuing in the communes of the 1960s, and later at places like Burning Man, is a liberation that proceeds by becoming ever more

oneself in the company of others. It's something where you are both more individualistic and more collaborative. This is a deeply liberal American mid-century idea, but it's fully alive now in the Valley. To be liberated, in the sense which the New Communalist wing meant it, was to be empowered by small-scale technologies, to pursue the transformation of your own consciousness, in the company of others. And that's very much what you see now in the Valley.

Increasingly, we wear these tools on our body. Is a biometric device like a Fitbit a tool of liberation or self-surveillance?

I think the liberated Californian is a person who is empowered and integrated into a system. In that context, surveillance is a powerful tool for self-improvement. We often think of surveillance as a tool in a kind of hierarchical state – and it can be, of course – but when you put on your Fitbit and log in, and see twenty other people who have logged in to their Fitbits, you are all watching each other and trying to help each other on your project of personal self-improvement. In that context, surveillance is not about power of others over you, it's the power of you to be more 'you' with others.

In the commune world, you might design an environment to build a better person and a better community. Part of the thrill of having an iPhone is not just how it feels in my hand, but that it connects me to a global system of others like myself. But, behind that, there's a backstage, a guy pulling strings. The pro-business turn set the stage for a world in which we take it as totally natural that private corporations should manage the platforms on which we interact, and through which we connect to one another. The countercultural imaginary was one in which there was no governing force, just information and feedback systems interacting with each other freely. We have a net today where we have beautiful handheld devices that make us feel free and empowered, but they connect us very directly to corporate entities with agendas very much their own. And that's one of the deep ironies of what the counterculture has become.

KEVIN KELLY

Interview by Brendan McGetrick

- Designing a process instead of a product
- The infinite productive power of amateurs
- Graphic design at Burning Man

In various ways, this exhibition asserts that the distinguishing feature of California design is its emphasis on personal liberation. To begin with, I'd like to hear your thoughts on that premise – whether you think that's accurate or perhaps too simplistic.

It's an interesting idea and actually one way to sum up my theory of technology, which is that it is primarily about creating more possibilities. David Eagleman describes it as a kind of religion of technology: not a belief in one God, but the belief in the expansion of possibilities of human potential, the expansion of human freedoms and choices. You can perceive the creation of the personal computer and the New Age human-potential movement as being basically the same thing, which is making possibilities for humans. So I think philosophically that is correct. What I have to think about is whether it's reflected in the creation, design and manufacturing of things.

One dimension of this phenomenon that we'd like to explore is the capacity of design and technology to stimulate the creation of new communities. You've been part of a number of projects that, in a way, invented new communities by combining groups that had previously existed independently and providing for them a new framework, in which they could see themselves and others as part of a single movement. Could you speak a bit about your experiences editing the *Whole Earth Catalog* in this context?

The *Whole Earth Catalog* was probably one of the original user-generated, peer-to-peer publishing ventures. What the *Whole Earth Catalog* ran was written by the readers with very little editing whatsoever, and at a rapid pace. It was like web blogging, but done on newsprint – and in that sense it preceded a lot of what we see on the Internet. It was inclusive because you needed almost no permission or credentials to participate, so the process part was very liberating.

Something I talk about in my book, *The Inevitable*, is the shift from products to processes, and what we will call California design is often not the product but the *process*. Many people have said – and I agree with them – that the greatest invention of Silicon Valley was not the transistor but actually the entrepreneurial process of making start-ups. That's the design innovation, so to speak. And one of the lessons of the current software regime of rapid prototyping and iterative revisions is that you do first and then you think. You don't design something by thinking about it and designing it perfectly.

For example, the Wikipedia publishing style is that you publish first and then you revise and edit it afterwards, rather than refining everything behind the scenes and then issuing the finished product. You put this unformed thing out and finish it with the help of the user, so it's co-created in that sense. That was seen originally as cheap, disreputable, almost cheating. But it turns out that this is the new process of making things: co-creation. There are problems with it, but I think this is part of the shift to a design process that is inclusive. The *Whole Earth Catalog* was one of the first to do that.

Another aspect of the *Whole Earth Catalog* was the fact that it was responsible in many ways for changing people's ideas about technology. The counterculture in the very beginning was very anti-technology in certain senses. Technology was seen as overpowering, in some ways monolithic, and not of a human scale. Stewart Brand came up with a slightly different take on it, which is that if you thought about technology as a system, you could see it like biology. It was organic – or it could be. Personal computers were evidence of technology on a human scale and organic, in a certain sense. The *Whole Earth Catalog*, which showed you how to build your own house and how to grow your own food, also had the very first personal computers, the HP programmable calculators. Over time, the *Whole Earth Catalog* was instrumental in changing people's minds about technology, to let them understand that technology could be organic and on a human scale – appropriate, we might say.

The other thing was that the catalogue was the *ur*-bible for 'do-it-yourselfers', not just tinkering in your basement but actually building your own house and making your own companies, starting your own businesses, home-schooling your own kids. It was, together with the other things that came up later on (Tinkering School, the Maker Movement, etc.), very much about this idea of empowering the individual or small group to make stuff and to make stuff happen. My website, Cool Tools, is an extension of that effort to enable individuals or small groups to tackle the most complicated things possible. The tools are now so much better, but you need to know that they exist. It's the power of the amateur, which oftentimes can

The premise was, 'I want to make a magazine that feels like it was mailed from the future.'

meet the power of the professional – particularly in a crowd.

The current thing is that all photographers are better than the best pro-photographer: you can find a better picture of the Golden Gate Bridge on Flickr than you can by hiring a pro. A pro will be better than the average amateur, but the pro's not better than all amateurs together. The *Whole Earth Catalog* was very instrumental in the rise of makers and the role that modification and making is now having on Californian culture.

Would you say that *Wired* magazine was an extension of the same impulse?
I think *Wired* was very much an extension – glossed up – of those things. It didn't have the 'do-it-yourself' aspect so much, although we emphasized the hacker/hacking stuff. There was more emphasis on celebrity, trying to make stars out of people, and less of the utilitarian, practical aspect. But, in terms of its sensibility and philosophy, I think it was an extension of *Whole Earth*. At least it was as far as when I was running it.

Whole Earth Catalog was founded in 1968; Wired in '93. How did the differences between the two publications reflect the differences in the culture at large at the time?

When *Wired* started, there was a new culture emerging with zines and the hacking of satellite radios; it was a communications and media revolution. There was a culture around technology, but it was not visible and the people doing it were dismissed as marginal. This was the genius of *Wired* as a commercial enterprise: they weren't just serving readers, but advertisers too, by making the argument that there's a group of people that is very influential, that has a lot of money and that nobody's talking to. *Wired*'s going to talk to them: initially, that was the premise. We were going to talk to this group that was making things and was at the frontier of a new culture.

Who were those people?
They were people playing video games, people who were online on the bulletin boards, the early adopters, the business people who were buying cell phones, the people who were hacking recording equipment, the musicians who were doing electronic music. It was very diverse, and that's why they weren't being reached. But we realized that they were actually all part of one big thing – we would call it a subculture now – and as soon as we started to articulate this vision, everybody else who was 'on the fence' suddenly got it too. Then, because it was being identified, it was

no longer marginal, and quickly became the centre of everything. Now there was a kind of framework, an ideology, a perspective, an identity – and that identity was *Wired*. That was the transition from the *Whole Earth Catalog*, which was unabashedly marginal: we were proud of the fact that we had thirty or forty thousand subscribers because they were very influential. Our belief was that by wrapping the stories around people and putting people – not technology – on the cover, we were going to raise its identity. And that's exactly what happened.

I suppose it's impossible to compare the early *Wired* with the current *Wired*, but I'm just curious – who do you think *Wired* speaks to now?

You know, it is hard because I don't know. *Wired* began as the pirate ship, and now it's become kind of the flagship. In the beginning it was very edgy – we didn't talk down or explain things, and people would open it up and be perplexed. They weren't exactly sure what we were talking about. The premise that Louis [Rossetto] sold, and which actually convinced me to work on the magazine, was 'I want to make a magazine that feels like it was mailed from the future'. That probably doesn't happen any more because the future is really online. It's almost impossible to compete against online venues entirely, so now it's more of a flagship. It presents the consensus and is authoritative. I think its function has changed: it appeals to a pretty broad audience, helping them keep on top of things and stay connected to the future.

How do you connect that effort to stay connected to the future, and to establish communities of people with similar interest, to your work with the Long Now Foundation?

One observation is that all the really great people thinking about the future, including a lot of science fiction authors, are huge history fans. You have to look back to see where things are going forward, particularly on an infrastructural level. The best science fiction authors are very good historians as well. Secondly, in order to do the big science-fiction-like projects that we all want requires the makers to take a longer viewpoint. You can't build and send a rocket to Mars if you're only concerned about the next quarter. You can't be concerned with paying off the stock price, even in a year or two. You have to say that this is going to take many, many decades. You might call it a non-market view – it's a longer-term view of the future that also requires a longer-term view of the past. That expansion away from the short, immediate now to the long now is part of what the Long Now Foundation is about. We make no claims that this is the business of business; we have a broader vision that says that to build a civilization that you're proud of, not everything should be derived from the market. You need to pay attention to other things, besides what will sell tomorrow. The pay-off may not be for many decades.

To conclude, I'd just like to return to your idea of design in California being more about process than product. Have you seen this concept expressed visually in any way?

I'll try to answer that, but before that I had another thought. Burning Man, which I'm a big supporter of, is for all intents and purposes a California event. I was a very regular goer for the early decades and have been documenting the Burning Man graphic style. I was going through all the camps and photographing the emerging graphic style, or even the architectural styles, that were appearing there. I've noticed that they were very reflective of the logos that would emerge from all those technology companies later on. When I think of a visual graphic style for California, I think of the Burning Man style. The thing that *Wired* invented was that colour was free, we decided to have five colours for everything, and the use of free, abundant colour was one of the graphic styles that emerged at that time. For me, the Burning Man style, with all the flags, banners and maker-made shelters, is really a California visual style.

So, going back to your question about visually representing those systems, one manifestation might be all of these innovation spaces that have tried to encourage openness and invention through architecture. Another example is IDEO, which has a design space with five little maxims painted on the wall, design maxims like 'Yes, and … ?'. These design or maker spaces like IDEO and the d.school at Stanford could be seen as a representation of this process, from the whiteboard to the stuff on the wall to the weird-shaped tables. In this sense, these spaces illuminate the design process by making the design process itself visible and tangible. They are the architecture of design process. Perhaps design process made visible is what California design is.

MATÍAS DUARTE

Interview by Justin McGuirk

- Silicon Valley before designers
- How Google is like Lego
- Designing software is all in the mind

When we first met, you were quite sceptical about the idea of California as a centre of design. Your instinctive reaction was that you had struggled with finding the designers you needed at Google in Silicon Valley. Can you explain why?

It's true. Software, for lack of a better term to describe the medium that Silicon Valley operates in, is very new. When we think of industrial design, there are processes and materials that are innovative – the plastics revolution, for instance – but so much stays the same. Now we have this whole category of things that we call devices – there used to be things, or maybe tools, and now we have devices. 'Device' means it has software, it has the ability to process, it probably has a user interface and a connection to the Internet. Software grew up in a very pragmatic 'can we just get things off the ground?' way. So there wasn't a lot of experience or talent around that understood the basic processes of design. I think video games actually absorbed a lot of the energy of people who were trying to do creative design with software, because they were interactive and tap into emotions, and because there's a question of story that comes into video games. But so many of the non-entertainment products that Silicon Valley is built on were very far from that in culture and attitude.

Design, as opposed to things that get categorized as engineering, is what touches the human experience. If you're building an aeroplane that is just going to haul cargo back and forth, the human experience is not prioritized. Once you get to passengers who are comfortable and enjoying the romance of air travel, then you start to consider everything about the human experience: the aesthetics, the comfort and the ergonomics. And so it's much like that, what we've seen in Silicon Valley. Throughout my career here, when I've tried to hire people who are really good at things like typography, graphic design, even things that are relatively new, like motion graphics, the talent wasn't here in Silicon Valley. Which is why for such a long time we saw this very naive expression in our software interfaces. There was almost an endearing primitivism to it. So I'd find myself hiring people from New York or Hollywood to do these things. But it's changing.

Speaking of endearing primitivism, until quite recently Google interfaces seemed to be self-consciously avoiding design.

Google was in a different state entirely, where it wasn't even trying. Over the last three to five years, we've started to bring in some of the last 2,000 years or so's practice of graphic arts and visual communication. But when I first joined Google, there was no understanding of the role of design, of the contribution to the complete solution of the problem that design could bring. There was no appreciation of this kind of human, personal experience.

So, at what stage does Google begin to value design?

I recall it happening maybe about six months after I joined. Maybe the fact that I was hired was some indication. I was hired by Andy Rubin, the founder of Android, which was getting ready for its sixth release. And at that time Google products were so unconsidered as to often end up hostile. I think even Larry [Page] and Sergey [Brin] were also starting to care about it. They had started to realize, 'We're trying to do more than just this search thing. We have all these products.' I think they became aware that not everybody loved everything, and they genuinely tried to understand why that was. What was it that their company was missing? I remember them being really keenly interested in how they could improve the design, and I don't think they really had a good understanding of everything that that implied at the time. But they were talking about it as though it was something that mattered.

You're head of something called Material Design. What does that mean?

Well, that came much later. After six more versions of Android, I started working on a project in concert with design leaders from across Google to come up with a design system that we would use across the company – which meant for Android, for the Web and for iOS as well. And then I thought, I rather like the sound of that; let's work on a design system that is actually encoding and making easy and useful for people all of the fundamentals of these software experiences, so people aren't having to start from scratch. And we ended up calling that Material Design. We rallied the company around that banner, updating tonnes of products across all these platforms. And when that was done, I went to Sundar [Pichai] because he became CEO at that point, and I said, 'If this is

One thing that's unique about software is that it has certain properties, like wood or steel or glass, and one of these properties is that it's constantly mutable and constantly evolving.

going to be an actual change at Google, we need to make this not just a mountain we climbed once and patted ourselves on the back for; we need to make this an ongoing effort, it needs to be a product – for all our developers and all the third parties that are hungry for things like this.'

So Material Design was partly about brand coherence but also a consistent experience across all of the products?

Let's come up with a new design system that's actually completely coherent, a cross-platform design system that supports the kind of brand that we want to have, that enables Search to evolve into the future of Search, and eventually assistance. Let's use that design system and actually redesign all the Google Apps across all their different form factors so they actually look like they came from a single team, not three different companies.

So, it's like a modular system, with the code built in, that you can deploy? Like building blocks; like Lego.

Like Lego! The code is like Lego. So the process is trying to give designers the tools that so many other working teams have. Programmers have all these tools for how they communicate, how they collaborate, how they comment, how they share

something. We want to give you tools to make those processes work the way designers work.

Why did you call it Material Design?

We were thinking about how we want designers to perceive it. We had a tagline for this thing – this as yet unnamed thing – as a system for rational space, form and motion. We were saying: all these three things are peers, they all need to be considered together, much like you would an industrial design of an object; this is the industrial design of software, and these are the fundamental building blocks. And let's just say it is a material. It doesn't matter what the material is. The metaphor is: think about appropriately designing with the material of software, in the same way that if you were learning to be an architect or an industrial designer, you would learn to design with the material of wood or steel or aluminium or whatever. That's where it came from.

It's an interesting choice of name because we tend to think of this new medium as immaterial.

Yes, but I think this is why software has been so bad for so long. Because, in reality, you can make those little blinking lights do whatever you want. But when you're learning to craft tools as an industrial designer, or craft spaces as an architect, the materials you use have very obvious constraints and properties. And learning to understand those constraints and properties is exactly what makes you a master in that space. And the funny thing is that when you come to designing software, it looks like there's no constraints – but that's wrong. Actually, there are very important constraints, and they're not in the code or in the screen. The constraints are all in your head, in your eyes, in billions of years of evolutionary biology that has formed our cognitive systems. Our material is actually in the mind.

What is it that makes software design unique as a medium?

One thing that's unique about software is that it has certain properties, like wood or steel or glass, and one of these properties is that it's constantly mutable and constantly evolving. It doesn't require someone to go back to the store to buy a better one, or someone to break one in order to have a window of opportunity to get a new one. It can be constantly evolving in reaction to your interactions, or to advances in technology. And that deeply influences the way that software is designed. It's intrinsically iterative, as you're trying to approach a better and better solution.

In many ways, that is one of the defining characteristics of design from California: this impatience to get a product out into the world so that it can be updated and improved. It's a new design methodology based on a culture of rapidly evolving tech products. Even Google's physical products follow that rhythm. Google Glass, for example, was out in the world without ever being made available.

Glass was never actually a product, it was only ever a developer toolkit. It was a prototype for developers to use. I think this is one of the things about Google's design culture, much like our self-driving cars. Because this company comes from a background in software, on the software side there's still a willingness to be transparent about the process. The company iterates in the public space. I don't think people understood Glass. I don't think people understood Glass as a developer product, as a thing that was in iteration, that nobody thought we should sell this, in the same way that I don't think people understand the self-driving cars that were driving around. This is not a consumer product that we're launching, this is a thing that we're doing because we think it's important to iterate. We're just having to tell you all about it because we're not the kind of company that thinks we can do our best work by hiding it. This is how Californian companies are starting to

think about it now. Tesla's doing the same thing with their autopilot. Their autopilot is not a self-driving car feature – it doesn't drive itself. But, by doing it publicly, and being willing to take all the PR flack when there are accidents with their autopilots, they're able to learn so much faster than if they were doing it secretly. That's a very Silicon Valley concept, this idea of user testing and user research: taking the products that you are in the process of building, and putting them in front of customers.

One of Google's most essential products is Maps. It's interesting to think about it as design. How is an online map a work of design?

Maps is actually to a certain degree a straightforward problem. The key insight is, it's a map. Focus on the map and then everything else kind of layers on top of it and sits at the periphery of it. But one of the things that the team did a lot of thinking on, particularly in this last update (the one that they called Tactile, where they made the map bleed to the edge of your browser), was what the map itself should look like. That means all the different ways that we could render information on the map, and the character it should have. How much should the map reflect the character of the brand, of Google, versus how much should the map try to reflect an impartial ground truth. There are very serious considerations, like 'what makes a map useful?' – in terms of information density, legibility and so forth. There are some fascinating intersections between design as concept and design as clever engineering: for instance, how you lay out street names on a map so they're not overlapping each other, and so that important street names are still visible from a distance.

These are highly technical designs, created by somebody who understood cartography in partnership with somebody who understood the engineering. It's not just the cartographer coming up with these rules – the design process is a partnership. At least two people, probably more. Software design requires teamwork, because the medium of software is not just a sea of ones and zeros – it's this very deep, layered stack of all these different expertises, and it's very rare to find people who have a skill set that spans that stack. But even if you did, to do anything at scale requires so much effort that you just can't do it yourself.

APRIL GREIMAN

Interview by Jennifer Dunlop Fletcher

- Creating 3D posters
- Technology as texture
- Finding inspiration in low resolution

You are originally from New York and studied in Kansas City and Basel. How did you land in Los Angeles, and what did you discover there?

I thought California would be more open politically, and, as a younger culture, more open-minded socially. I thought I'd go for about six months, but then discovered the desert and made Los Angeles my home.

I remember saying to friends, 'The bad thing about LA is there's no culture yet.' It didn't have a strong design thrust except for the modernist period. Overall, it was just a free-for-all. The bad part was that it lacked tradition, which coincidentally was the great thing. I revelled and prospered in LA's openness. California graphics made a big splash internationally, and I got a little bit of notoriety as a very green young woman in LA with work in lots of publications. It was too much too soon.

So from like '78 or '79, the shit really hit the fan for me. People were saying my work was too personal, and it's garbage. This wasn't coming predominantly from Europe or Asia – in fact, there couldn't be enough praise or enough interest in it from those quarters. It was coming from the East Coast: somebody saying, 'She just stands at the top of the stairs and throws type down, and wherever it lands is what gets printed.' This couldn't be further from the truth, because even at that time I always used a grid. Diagonal type can go on a grid. But it was very painful for me that people said to go back to fine art. It made me wildly uncomfortable, I was really suffering.

So the dean of the art school at CalArts, who hired me to head the graphic design programme, noted my suffering, and he asked whether there were other media I always wanted to work in. And I said, 'Yes, I've always been interested in video because I am interested in the third and fourth dimensions. I've always wanted sound in my work.'

To a certain extent, graphics, being a print medium, was very limiting for me, and I'd pushed it as far as I could. I had used Day-Glo print, and designed a 3D poster viewed with 3D glasses, and I was always pushing new experiences with type. And so he set me up with someone in the film/

video school. At night, I would go there and start working with one-inch video equipment. It was SONY equipment, it was set up with a synthesizer and an analogue computer – and so I was using this equipment and shooting objects and things in motion and capturing them on the computer, and working with, of course, somebody who was very fluent in the technology. I got the bug and even bought the first half-inch professional equipment, which allowed me to embed my own video images that I would shoot off a monitor with a high-quality camera. A friend of a friend introduced me to Paint Box, which, at the time, was only used by the television broadcasters and cost about $500–700 an hour to use because it was the entertainment business – that's the kind of money they had to throw at creative work. So I had a friend who freelanced in all the post-production facilities. I would work between midnight and six a.m., when no one was using it. And it was so much fun.

I want to circle back to the use of video images in graphic design. Is it important that your work reveal the DNA of the technology behind it, through a pixelated image?

Not necessarily – so, with the Paint Box application and equipment, you use two monitors simultaneously. One is broadcast, which is the big monitor, where you get everything TV-sized or film-sized, and the small monitor is high definition. The broadcasters had their creative department do two sets of exactly the same thing. One would go out to broadcast, and then a high-resolution version would go to print. I was never really interested in everything having a pixel revealed in it, I didn't want to use high-end photography to make a seamless image of something. I wanted to reveal the state-of-the-art – ride the horse in the direction it's going. Either jump on the train or jump in front of the train. I was trained in type, I know quality. But why bury the process? Why make it look like something it isn't? Why be embarrassed; why not find out a way to communicate and educate about technology? For me, there was a texture there. I think texture brings out emotion in people. Literally, you have a different feeling if you're touching a piece of satin than when you're touching very rough concrete. I think that's important – the hand-eye coordination, and the mind-body coordination. I'm a sensual being.

Since technologies have evolved so much in the past twenty years, have you found yourself riding along with the latest, as you said, or did you get off at a certain point and say I'm going to stick with this one?

Oh, I've been riding the horse. I have my own ways of keeping my hands dirty and my feet on the

I remember saying to friends, 'The bad thing about LA is there's no culture yet.'

ground. I've had one of the best digital imagers saying they wouldn't work with me because I submitted a file that was only seventy-two dpi for a large-scale image, and they just said it would be an embarrassment to work with me, and yet they did it. One of my images was fourteen dpi and for me, it was a moving painting. I didn't want to call them photographs, I wanted to call them digital paintings.

You and I have had conversations about this, as we discovered the medium description on a work on view at SFMOMA. The actual medium was an offset lithograph, and yet that doesn't differentiate it from earlier works. You feel it is important for the viewer to know more about the process and tools.

Right, it was so unfair.

As some technologies become 'sunset', the understanding of how a work was made gets lost. It is becoming increasingly important to spell out processes, especially what techniques and technologies were used.

It pained me, when I saw the label; I was just devastated, thinking, 'Holy cow, without knowing the process, the work doesn't make sense.' The irony is that the work is called 'Does it Make Sense?' I'm just an explorer and I've never cared what it was called, until it was incorrect. It's nobody's fault, but it's been painful to me, because it diminishes what I've explored and what I've been willing to do, on my own time. It's not always great but it's what I love to do. I want people to learn something from what I do. I try new things and I learn so much, and that's the fun for me: kind of jumping into the void and seeing what happens. I don't have

preconceived ideas or media I work with. I like a playpen – a big open field and space.

Here is your opportunity: what would be the ideal medium for 'Does it Make Sense?'?

It's video computer graphic, because it's video that's run through the computer, and output on a dot-matrix printer. And then offset printed. It's a video-computer-offset-lithograph.

How were you bringing video into the piece itself? Were you still using the camera and then scanning?

There's a little piece of technology that costs a thousand bucks, which I spent my entire honorarium from the Walker *Design Quarterly* budget on. It was a little box that had two cables out – one went to your video equipment and the other one directly into your computer, so it automatically scans your video. It went directly into the Mac. And then from there, you output to your printer, which at the time was dot-matrix, low-resolution printing. And then I printed it out; at that time all you could print on was letter-sized paper, so that got printed out on letter-sized bond paper, and I tiled it out.

We've talked about how important it is to reveal the technologies, but you are also the subject of the work. Do you consider this a self-portrait?

Yeah, I guess I do. Actually, of course I do. That was the day that a suffering graphic designer would be against the very established New York male designer population. So I put my body in there to punctuate the human, female struggle over the chronology of time. Yes, it's a portrait. And if you think things went smoothly after that, it was one of the most successful things I've done to put myself out of business.

Switching scales to the very large mural, 'Hand Holding a Bowl of Rice' (2007), let's speak about the migration of your design into space – the spatial aspect of the design, which we touched on a little bit in regards to typography.

Somehow I got some early breaks, in the early 2000s, to do some public art. And so, luckily, I got the commission. I was recommended to Urban Partners by an art consultant. I guess she felt I was familiar with deadlines and budgets, and making presentations with my professional design background. I worked for twenty-plus years with architects in the built environment, doing colour and signage and other three-dimensional work. So 'Hand Holding a Bowl of Rice' is really the quintessential hybrid for transmedia work I've done.

It is monumental in scale. Please talk about the processes behind it.

The first thing I did was get the model. I really consider it part of the building rather than something attached, like a sign. I wanted to integrate the whole city block. It was going to be the entrance to a metro station. I started shooting video. That's usually my go-to tool: shooting video or photography. So I drove day and night, shot video of the whole area. It's in Korea Town; I was looking for context and still images and so forth. One thing that struck me about Korea Town versus any other place in LA was that Korea Town is actually a 24/7 part of town. You can get a bowl of noodles at three in the morning. I also wanted a symbol for this particular culture that is really strong. It's the largest population of Koreans outside of Korea. And so I started just researching symbolism, and thinking about that, and I stumbled on an exhibition on rice. The bowl of rice, or rice, symbolizes abundance, and I thought it'd be really interesting to capture video image of a hand holding a bowl of rice. There's no rice and you can barely see the bowl, it's more just an object – a bowl being held. So that's the image I chose, and I thought it was really good that it was in Korea Town, for the Asian communities. It was kind of a welcome symbol into not only the building but to the neighbourhood.

Would a live-feed video project interest you? 'Hand Holding a Bowl of Rice' was originally conceived as a live-feed project but needed to be scaled back for various reasons. Does live feed still sound appealing, maybe for another project?

Oh sure. One idea I've had is to project feed from a phone on to a large-scale surface, like a building wall. And you would see the image or

video in high definition on the phone, and simultaneously you could be seeing the lowest definition on the building's surface. So you see kind of the texture of technology with these single strands running thirty feet (nine metres) vertically in a square formation.

Returning to the subject of California – what keeps you in California? Is it the specific industries there? Is it the like-minded community? Is there a California ethos or approach? Or a California or LA perspective?

It's light and space. That's it.

How is the light and space different in California?

I discovered the desert. That's where light and space has its greatest influence over me, and brings out the best in me. And like what Joni Mitchell said about Los Angeles: they've taken the desert and covered it with a parking lot. When I'm in Los Angeles, I still live in the desert, I'm in the desert all the time, and it's just such a nourishment for me. It's an inspiration and it gives me plenty of opportunities to personally and professionally pursue ... just to explore light and space, and see how it influences the colour.

You feel like there's a broader range in colour than elsewhere?

Oh, totally. I think it has the most beautiful light. There are other places, like Jerusalem, that has the same light because it's desert. Although it's more golden there than it is here. Paris has incredible light. It's much cooler. But there's a warmth here that just gets to my bones. I feel grounded here, and I feel like when all else fails, or if I'm feeling down, this light revives me. Even when it's raining here, there's a quality of light. I've just never found other places like that; I haven't found other places where I can do the work I do. It's one thing to go and live in Morocco and get that light all day, but I have an overhead. So we have a place that is the desert – and that's a treasure of inspiration, rejuvenation and restoration.

And the expansiveness of the space is also inspiring or calming?

Oh yeah, light and space. The vastness of space, including mental space, is critical. I'm swimming in openness here.

DAVID KELLEY

Interview by Jennifer Dunlop Fletcher

- How compromise endangers designers
- IDEO's human factor
- Bringing European design to Silicon Valley

You were educated both in engineering and product design – was this unusual at the time? Why did you feel it was important to learn both?

I grew up enamoured with technological cleverness. My heroes were Thomas Edison, Eli Whitney and Alexander Graham Bell. I didn't really know what design was. I was in industrial Ohio; if I had been raised in Milan or London, I probably would have gone right into design. I was interested in how you realize inventiveness, and that led me to engineering. Unfortunately, it was a purely technical world, and too analytical; it wasn't creative enough for me. And so, when I found design, which valued a human-centred approach beyond function, it felt right. At Stanford, I didn't have to give up my undergraduate technical training that I received at Carnegie Mellon. Stanford combined the engineering school and art department together, so it was a particularly good fit for me. Without abandoning engineering, I gained design methodology and sensitivity. There weren't many places that combined industrial design and art at the time.

How did you land in California? Was it only the Stanford programme, or did you have an idea of California that also attracted you?

No, I didn't consider California for one second. It was Stanford. I'll quickly tell you the story. One of my closest friends from my time at Boeing kept badgering me – 'You gotta go to Stanford.' I didn't know what Stanford was; I knew my grades were poor, but he just badgered me until I applied. I didn't know it was going to be such a good fit for me, so it could have been in Timbuktu. It had nothing to do with Silicon Valley, or anything Californian.

A few years after you arrived here, you seemed to sense that something was missing. You were still drawn to the works of Italian designers for Olivetti. Why was it important to bring European design to Silicon Valley?

I started teaching at Stanford in 1978, and I started my company (which would later become IDEO) in 1978, and I was still loving design, but I wasn't really doing industrial design, in the same vein as the Eameses, Raymond Loewy or Henry Dreyfuss, or any of the European industrial designers. I was basically the person who didn't allow other people's designs to be compromised. So, at the time, the designers – Ettore Sottsass, or whoever else I was working with – would do these fabulous designs for other companies, but by the time it got into production – after the engineers and company had compromised the important bits away – the designers were no longer happy with the design, and so I saw it as my role as the design-sensitive engineering person to find a way to keep all the exciting parts of the design by being clever about how it could be made. I was really endeared to the designers because I cared so much about design. When we would do a project jointly, I was not threatening as a design person at all – I was the person who enabled them. Look at the Enorme phone we did with Sottsass. The box says 'Designed by Ettore Sottsass, engineered in California by David Kelley.' So, we did design and creative engineering.

You've been surrounded by this network of technology and engineering in the Bay Area that gave you early access to new digital tools. Now that we're looking back over twenty-five years at a very rapid evolution of design tools, what is your go-to design tool? And what technologies have really influenced how you design or work?

I'm glad to talk to you about tools. You remind me that the best part of it was that it was a new frontier – the tools were new, and the things we designed were new. It's fabulous to design something new because you get to innovate. If we were designing bicycles, they've been worked over for tens, if not hundreds, of years, and so to do an interesting bicycle you've got a lot of history to deal with, and somebody's probably already thought of any design contribution you could add. These objects are played out in some ways, but when you are designing a mouse for a computer or the first laptop – which we got to do, of course – you can make every decision. For example, we hold the patent on the laptop display closing over the keyboard to protect itself. Well, I would bet that almost anybody who designed it would have come up with that. Maybe not, but it was so exciting to do because nobody had worked that particular problem before! It was so exciting; it was like being in 'Star Trek' – we were inventing the future. And the tools were the same way – they were new to the world as well.

These tools were not even that widely adopted yet. Not that many designers were using software.

A person might say, 'I'm so stupid, I can't see how it works,' and we were really clear that the person wasn't stupid, but instead the designer had failed.

When we started using CAD machines, I remember – I probably still have our rate sheet – that if you wanted a designer, it was, like, $25 an hour. But if you wanted us to use a CAD machine, it was $25 an hour for the designer plus $20 an hour for the CAD machine. The tool was so whiz-bang, and the quality was considerably better. With CAD designs, you could try so many different iterations, which became part of our design process. You try things, but you still do it with intention, which is design. The more iterations you do, the better the design. The CAD machine allowed us – on a magnitude – to easily iterate and refine better than before.

I could see how this could also be liberating from the notion of 'design genius'.

CAD was one of those tools that still allowed for personal expression; the tool didn't take over in the design process. Look at a Frank Gehry building – a human couldn't do the geometry on those designs!

How and why was IDEO founded?

David Kelley Design started in 1978, right out of my time at Stanford, and we were this creative engineering company. Engineers wouldn't have called us engineers because we were not analytical enough – we were too hands-on, we were more like grubby mechanics. I also fell in love with this guy, Bill Moggridge, who really taught me a lot about design. Here was a European who got an early inkling about Silicon Valley; he was the guy who did understand that Silicon Valley was where the most interesting design was going to happen. He moved his family here lock-stock-and-barrel, because he wanted to design the future. So, he

and I hit it off with a major friendship right away. In 1991, we formed IDEO. Bill came up with the name. He looked in the dictionary and saw 'ideo-': the prefix for words like 'ideology', and so we thought it would be a clever branding prefix like what McDonalds does with McNuggets, Mc-this, Mc-that. But that never came to be, and IDEO ended up standing alone. It turned out that we didn't care about growing the business just for financial gain. We cared about getting more interesting projects than anybody else, and so it was a good name.

Did you start out with clearly defined roles or did you acknowledge the collaboration early on? Did you always start every project by throwing Post-it notes on the board?

Yes, we called it 'Human Factors' at the time. And that happened maybe five or six years earlier than IDEO. We were doing design, but we noticed that we were getting our big ideas from understanding human behaviour. My mentor at Stanford, Bob McKim, wrote a book, which was never published, called *Need Finding* that explored the notion that it was more important to find the problem worth working on, instead of solving the obvious one. And that became our methodology. We would identify what people really valued so we could do a good design, but it wasn't very formal. In the '90s, we figured out that we needed to hire anthropologists and sociologists for the crucial 'Need Finding' phase. Human-centred design really started to take off when we realized it differentiated us from more business- or engineering-focused firms.

Can you tell me about two or three career-shifting projects – successes or failures – that pushed you in new and exciting directions?

It's hard to tell the same story all the time, but for me it was Apple. There is no question. My company's work for Apple was in the late 1970s – long before IDEO. In fact, Apple made my company. I met Steve Jobs through a Stanford friend, who was working there when the Apple II had just been released. We started designing for Apple and did fifty-three projects early on. Everybody was asking Apple who was doing their design work because the company was such a phenomenon. And they said us! So, everybody was knocking on our door, asking us to do what we were doing for Apple. It was like drinking from a fire hose – there was no way we could keep up with demand.

Did you believe in Apple's vision, or was it just another successful company? Did you sense that everyone would soon have a personal computer on his or her desk, or did it seem far-fetched?

Oh sure! I definitely bought into the fact that the personal computer was really important – I mean *really* important. It felt as important as the automobile must have felt in the 1900s. There was no hesitancy – I mean, I'm in Silicon Valley, right?! Maybe if I had been in London or some sceptical place, it might have been different. No, we knew this was heading in a new, positive direction.

Was there something you saw in Apple that indicated how widely adopted the personal computer would become?

Apple recognized that personal computers were the future. There were plenty of computers, but any time you take something industrial and make it personal, it becomes super interesting. The computer phenomenon was realized because of Apple. It was certainly a turning point in computers, and it was centred on design. The important thing we learned about design from Jobs was to do every component with intention. Jobs mandated that we consider all aspects of the experience, from the first time you see the box, the first time you open it, to the first time you turn on the computer. He specified that the interface design was as important as the hardware. From a business standpoint, there is no question that our relationship with Apple helped our company, but more importantly, attitudinally, it expanded our approach. From then on, we were designing the product and the experience around the product.

Can you describe that shift further?

We never let go of designing the hardware, but we expanded our scope, which made the

design discipline grow. Moggridge is central in this. He would say interface is way too important to leave to the technologists. 'We gotta get in there.' We started to realize, years after the Apple thing, that if we were going to 'delight the user', we had to use storytelling to paint a picture of the future with the product in it. If I designed a cell phone in the old way, I'd make a model. It would be beautiful. I'd put it under a black cloth and when the CEO came in, I'd pull up the cloth and say, 'Look!' and everyone would go, 'Wow!' We started to realize that it wasn't enough and so we shifted towards painting a picture of the object's use and potential – the human/computer interaction. Moggridge wrote the seminal book on interactive design. Being in Silicon Valley, it became clear that human/computer interaction was necessary to be relevant for people's lives. And the people developing the technology weren't particularly good at that, but as designers and humanists we recognized the use of new objects would need to be obvious at first glance.

Bill and I had a lot of empathy for our users, which was insightful. A person might say, 'I'm so stupid, I can't see how it works', and we were really clear that the person wasn't stupid, but instead the designer had failed. This really drove us to the whole human-centred approach. We kept seeing things happen that we knew were significant because the user was stressed. It started to feel really good when we fixed those problems because they were human problems.

In your view, is there a California perspective or attitude in design?

Yes, I think that being in California – and I'm talking about Northern California; I can't speak to Southern California – there is a vitality to the place, there is a positive vibe. Oh, now I sound like I'm from California, don't I? Hey, I'm from Ohio – but there is such a positive outlook and shared recognition that the future is being designed here. We're in Silicon Valley, in the Bay Area, and the notion that we can change the world together is really energizing. Every start-up I know has a designer in it. We're a strategic weapon. Companies recognize that a design mentality is important in order to routinely innovate. The competitiveness seen elsewhere is regressive because it only achieves personal gain. Here, there is an embarrassment of riches – and competition is less of a worry. Rather, there is a community grateful to be in the place where the future is being invented successfully.

YVES BÉHAR

Interview by Jennifer Dunlop Fletcher

- Why the best tools are pencil and paper
- AI as the next dimension of design
- Designing for product categories that don't exist

Please describe your design education. What is your impression of that education in hindsight, or even in the moment?

I studied design at the Art Center College of Design – two years at its Swiss campus and two years at its Los Angeles campus. Design education in the late 1980s/early 1990s viewed the designer as a decorator – someone hired by companies for determining an aesthetic element. I felt, even back then, the designer should be a conceptual collaborator on all aspects of a project. To me, the design process and outcome is equivalent to film-making and other modes of storytelling. I loved Art Center because all art and design disciplines shared the same building so I was able take classes in the other areas – including film, photography and graphic design – which helped expand how I conceptualized and represented design.

Having grown up in Switzerland, was Art Center also attractive because it had a campus in California? Did you have a preconceived notion of California and its approach to design when you started school there?

Art Center does typify California. Instead of viewing design as applied marketing, Art Center certainly exemplified a Californian future thinking, future dreaming. Also, Californian culture is outdoors in nature. As a Swiss boy, who grew up on the shore of a lake, Art Center and California were exciting because they were focused on both nature and future as horizons to explore deeply in design.

And what kept you in California? Was it really the proximity to surf and snow, or were you also aware of the robust engineering, technology and space sectors?

Honestly, California felt like an invitation to me; my skills and ideas were welcome and encouraged. There was a progressive culture in California that invited collaboration. When I started to interview in San Francisco for jobs, I was immediately struck by how diverse, how international, it was. American industrial design felt a bit stuck. Technology offered the opportunity for us to expand design's capacity. So, the combination of plenty of jobs, inclusion of people from other places and openness to new ideas – all these were irresistible to a European designer like me.

I've noticed you are quite invested in design's potential to change staid behaviours. Are there any objects or designers who were influential in shaping this perspective?

In my early twenties, I was an intern at Steelcase in Michigan, which was close to Herman Miller's headquarters, and where I spent some time looking at the archives of Charles and Ray Eames. There are so many great Eames projects, but maybe the one that matters the most to me is the Eames Rocker. It was conceived in the late 1940s and it adds a new, playful dimension to the traditional formality of the living room, and the house itself. It completely changes the way that people converse with each other, offering freedom from social convention. So, it made me realize very early on that products have the ability to change people's attitude and preconceived notions, and inspire new behaviour. Design can inspire how we live, how we relate to each other and how we experience things. Rather than furthering tradition, which is a very European Swiss thing to think about, the Eames Rocker opened up a sense that there is more than one approach, and that we are constantly evolving. Design can foster that perspective. Design celebrates the adoption of new ideas – for social interactions and for business transactions – and design makes that new attitude accessible.

Most of your products are mass-produced and widely accessible, and simply at this scale provide opportunity for greater social change. Did you consider the potential of working in this scale from your time at Steelcase and Herman Miller?

Absolutely. I've always wanted to bring new ideas to as many people as possible.

Since you arrived in California, design tools, engineering and technology have rapidly evolved. Of all the technologies you've worked with in the past twenty-five years or so, what is your go-to design tool for initial concepts? What technologies fit best with your practice?

Pencil and paper – they're still the fastest way to take ideas that reside in your brain and put them on paper for people to understand. That said, the next stage for us is a 3D-printed model, which is probably the technology we use the most. The ability to iterate in three dimensions has given us control over the development of the form

In the last ten years, I've noticed that technology also expands intelligence – in particular, artificial intelligence and robotics – which also create a whole new dimension in design.

throughout the entire process. You used to have to transfer this information to someone else, who would then carry that along to production.

Pencil and paper are still the quickest way for you to express an initial concept, but it seems the ability to iterate in 3D-printed prototypes has been the most beneficial digital tool for your design process. Is that fair to summarize?

So, we do software typing and iteration by hand, sketching or sculpting foam or other material, but that same iteration process can happen in parallel. Once we have a model drawn in 3D, we can machine it and 3D-print it. Client and public interest in process is new; before, people only wanted to see the finished product or the glossiest rendering, and today they are fascinated with the changes and refinements from concept to production. From a visit to the Eames archive, it was immediately apparent how every iteration either closes the door on a project or opens up a new range of possibilities. Today, instead of carving pieces of wood, we do it very efficiently and quickly through 3D-printing and machining.

I hear your appreciation for digital tools that allow quicker refinement, but I want to return to the broader vision of design that you spoke of earlier.

Are there new digital media that expand the design experience beyond product hardware?

In the last ten years or so, I've noticed that technology also expands intelligence – in particular, artificial intelligence and robotics – which also create a whole new dimension in design. I often equate two-dimensional design with graphic design, three-dimensional design with industrial design. Merging the two into a single, three-dimensional product with an interface, and then layering AI or robotics, in a smart environment, we suddenly enter the fourth dimension – time. How do things evolve and change over time? How do they get better? How do the products and experiences we work on improve and transform and accompany us for longer periods of time in our lives? Time as a dimension means we consider a varied user experience, whether it's on a mobile device or a computer screen – you have to know how the project is communicated, understood and used. We have to ensure that all the features and functions are legible and connected, in order to deliver a consistent experience.

I've noticed that you and your team are committed to understanding the total experience, and to trying prototypes out as part of your daily lives. I was thinking about the new Snoo crib in particular,

and how many of your staff members have taken it home and tested it out on their newborns.

If we think that the human experience is at the centre of new products and new designs, we then seek ways to test how we think they will be useful. Quite often, because of a confidentiality agreement, we test them on ourselves. We're lucky to have a diverse and large staff pool – but, fundamentally, we believe in these ideas, which reduces the risk factor. It was the same with the public-office landscape we were designing for Herman Miller. There, we worked for a whole year with cardboard prototypes of the furniture and arrangements we were designing. Progressively, our experience allowed us to refine the system all the way until we had a full seventy-five-person final prototype, which we used for a year, launching the final product with Herman Miller. Since we design a lot of 'firsts', prototyping and understanding our response and usage are really important. Snoo is the first 'smart' bassinet, Up is the first wearable health tracker, Jambox is the first Bluetooth speaker, and so we can't test them on the outside world until we refine the design so that even though the product may be unknown, the experience is logical and seamless. So, in order to create a holistic experience of something entirely new, it's quite healthy to have a diverse team from different practices, from different places around the world, and from different cultures. San Francisco is a perfect place for designing and building 'firsts'.

It's rare that a designer is also a business partner – especially in so many different companies. Please speak about the importance and value of investing in many of your design projects so completely.

Early on, it was clear to me that the best designs are the ones that are a result of a long-term relationship with a company. The more you work on something, the more you understand it, the better it gets. And for me, a partnership that supports the development of expertise, and commits to a long-term vision and then sets about achieving it, is critical to good design. A great design only increases the value of the company.

Please tell me about two or three career or practice-shifting projects – ones that took your practice in a new direction, or felt like they really brought together all the goals you laid out.

There are three or four moments in the last sixteen years or so that have changed, transformed or accelerated our practice. One Laptop per Child really made it possible for a computer to survive and to thrive in a completely different environment. That project made technology interesting again. We were able to meet and observe a variety of learners in such different environments; it was a giant eye-opener.

Another significant project was the Sayl chair with Herman Miller. It is the result of about ten years of work with Herman Miller, which allowed for a new approach to design innovation, fabrication and materials that had not been seen in chairs before. The Sayl chair is the lowest-cost chair that Herman Miller offers. It's manufactured on three continents, and is very well understood across cultures – across Asia, across Europe, across the US – which is a sign of success. People around the world are responding positively to its functionality, the ergonomics and the smaller scale.

The third big moment happened in two phases, ten years apart: the advance of wearables. It all started with a commission by SFMOMA to design a shoe for the future, and I designed the learning shoe. The shoe had sensors to learn from the user, and that data would be used to make a new pair for the user for improved performance or health. And that was at a time when Bluetooth and Wi-Fi didn't exist.

Since then, I have continued to work on wearables – headsets for mobile communication; watches; and, with the availability of Bluetooth, we released the Up Band health monitor. Bluetooth allowed for immediate feedback and communication. Your experience of the product is personalized; it's your activity patterns, your lifestyle choices. So many people tell us how this feedback supported major life changes they wanted to make by revealing habits they couldn't see before. In many ways, the data was the big reveal of things that they weren't even aware of, things that they did every day. The minimalization of how small the product was, how integrated it is in everyday life, all those things really were stepping stones for wearables and wearable technology. So then, the Up Band was a 'first' also – it was the first tracker that would give you sleep information; it was the first one on your wrist; and, in many ways, it was a precursor to many other projects we continue to work on today – including the Superflex Power Clothing device that we've just presented in London.

Do you think there's a California perspective, attitude or approach in design? Do you ever speak with colleagues about such an approach? Is there a Northern California approach?

Absolutely. I think there is a pioneering spirit in California that benefits designers every day. Today, there is a conviction that designers are an intrinsic part of any new business and the introduction of any new technology. Designers in Northern California are very fortunate to be in such a healthy environment that breeds new ideas.

Yves Béhar   219

AFTERWORD

Talk by Steve Jobs
at the International
Design Conference
in Aspen, 1983, with
an introduction by
Jonathan Ive

JONATHAN IVE

In 1983 Steve Jobs spoke at the International Design Conference in Aspen. As well as predicting the ubiquity of computers at a time when most people had never even used one, he called on designers to play their part in making computers part of everyday life. Here, Jonathan Ive, Chief Design Officer of Apple, introduces Jobs's talk, recalling a visionary, an educator and a friend.

Steve rarely attended design conferences. This was 1983, before the launch of the Mac, and still the relatively early days of Apple. I find it breathtaking how profound his understanding was of the dramatic changes that were about to happen as the computer became broadly accessible. Of course, beyond just being prophetic, he was fundamental in defining the products that would change our culture and our lives forever.

On the eve of launching the first truly personal computer, Steve is not solely preoccupied with the founding technology and functionality of this new category. He is deeply concerned about the product's design. This is extraordinarily unusual, as in the early stages of dramatic innovation, it is normally the primary technology that benefits from all of the attention and focus.

Steve points out that the design effort in the US at that time had been focused on the automobile, with little consideration or effort given to consumer electronics. While it is not unusual to hear leaders talk about the national responsibility to manufacture, I thought it was interesting that he talked about a nation's responsibility to design.

In the talk, Steve predicts that by 1986 sales of the PC would exceed sales of cars, and that in the following ten years, people would be spending more time with a PC than in a car. These were absurd claims for the early 1980s. Describing what he sees as the inevitability that this would be a pervasive new category, he asks the designers in the audience for help. He asks that they start to think about the design of these products, because designed well or designed poorly, they still would be made.

Steve remains one of the best educators I've ever met in my life. He had that ability to explain incredibly abstract, complex technologies in terms that were accessible, tangible and relevant. You hear him describe the computer as doing nothing more than completing fairly mundane tasks, but doing so very quickly. He gives the example of running out to grab a bunch of flowers and returning by the time you could snap your fingers — the speed rendering the task magical.

The revolution Steve described over thirty years ago did of course happen, and California has grown to become the home of so many companies that shape our culture and the ways we work and communicate.

I moved to this area very specifically to join Apple but have come, like Steve, to love it. What is it about Silicon Valley that could support and nurture so many companies that would have such a profound impact on the world? Obviously there is the momentum of large groups of people attracting like-minded individuals. There's the infrastructure that is both physical and social. But for some, it also has something to do with the light. I adore the nature of the light here and the view of the mountains that you see when you are down in the valley.

STEVE JOBS

**Edited transcript of a talk at the International
Design Conference in Aspen, 1983**

Introductions are really funny. They paid me sixty
dollars so I wore a tie.

How many of you are over thirty-six years
old? You were born pre-computer. Computers
are thirty-six years old. I think there's going to be
a little slice in the timeline of history as we look
back, a pretty meaningful slice right there. A lot of
you are products of the television generation. I'm
pretty much a product of the television generation,
but to some extent starting to be a product of the
computer generation. But the kids growing up now
are definitely products of the computer generation,
and in their lifetimes the computer will become the
predominant medium of communication, just as
the television took over from the radio, took over
from even the book …

How many of you own an Apple? Any? Or just
any personal computer? How many of you have
used one, or seen one, or anything like that?

OK, let's start off with what a computer is.
It's just a simple machine. But it's a new type
of machine. The gears, the pistons, have been
replaced with electrons. How many of you have
seen an electron? The problem with computers is
that you can't get your hands on the actual things
that are moving around – you can't see them – and
so they tend to be very intimidating because in
a very small space there's billions of electrons
running around and we can't really get a hold on
exactly what they look like. Computers are very
adaptive. We can move the electrons around
differently to different places, depending upon the
current state of affairs, the results of the last time
we moved the electrons around. So if you were
here last night and you heard about how the brain
is very adaptive, a computer is in the same way
very adaptive.

The second thing about a computer is that
it's very new. It was invented thirty-six years ago, in
1947. The world's first degree in computer science
was a master's degree offered by the University of
California at Berkeley, in 1968, which means the
oldest person who has such a degree is thirty-nine
years old. And the average age of professionals
at Apple is under thirty. So, it's a field that's domi-
nated by young people.

The third thing about computers is that
they're really dumb. They're exceptionally simple,
but they're really fast. The raw instructions that we
have to feed these little microprocessors – or even
these giant Cray-1 supercomputers – are the most
trivial of instructions. They get some data from
there, get a number from here, add two numbers
together and test to see if it's bigger than zero. It's
the most mundane thing you could ever imagine.
But here's the key thing: let's say I could move a
hundred times faster than anyone in here. In the
blink of your eye, I could run out there, grab a
bouquet of fresh, spring flowers, run back in here
and snap my fingers. You would all think I was a
magician. And yet, I would basically be doing a
series of really simple instructions: running out
there, grabbing some flowers, running back,
snapping my fingers. But I could just do them so
fast that you would think that there was something
magical going on, and it's the exact same way with
a computer. It can do about a million instructions
per second. And so we tend to think there's something magical going on, when in reality it's just a
series of simple instructions. Now what we do is
take a collection of these very simple instructions
and build a higher-level instruction. So, instead
of saying, 'Turn right, left foot, right foot, left foot,
right foot, extend hand, grab flowers, run back in,'
I can say, 'Could you go get some flowers?' And we
have started in the last twenty years to deal with
computers in higher and higher levels of abstraction. But ultimately, these levels of abstraction get
translated down into these stupid instructions that
run really fast.

Let's look at the brief history of computers.
The best way to understand it is probably by way
of analogy. Take the electric motor. When it was
first invented in the late 1800s, it was only possible
to build a very large one, which meant it could
only be cost-justified for very large applications.
Electric motors therefore did not proliferate very
fast at all. But, the next breakthrough was when
somebody took one of these large electric motors
and ran a shaft through the middle of the factory,
and through a series of belts and pulleys, shared
the horsepower of this one large electric motor
in fifteen or twenty medium-sized workstations,
thereby allowing one electric motor to be cost-
justified on some medium-scale tasks. And electric
motors proliferated even further then. The real
breakthrough was the invention of the fractional-
horsepower electric motor. We could then bring
the horsepower directly to where it was needed,
and cost-justify it on a totally individual application.
I think there's about fifty-five or so fractional-horsepower electric motors in every household now.

If we look at the development of computers,
we see a real parallel. The first computer was called
the ENIAC, in 1947. It was developed particularly for

ballistic, military calculations. It was giant, hardly anybody got a chance to use it. The next real breakthrough was in the sixties with the invention of what was called 'timesharing'. What we did was take one of these very large computers, and shared it. Since it could execute so many instructions so quickly, we'd run some on Fred's job over here, and then we'd run some on Sally's job, and then we'd run some on Don's job. It was so fast that everybody thought they had the computer to themselves. Timesharing was what really started to proliferate computers in the sixties – and most of you, if you've used computer terminals, are connected with some umbilical cord to some large computer somewhere else. That's timesharing. That's what got computers on college campuses in large numbers.

The reason Apple exists is because we stumbled on to fractional-horsepower computing five years before anyone else. That's the reason we exist. We took these microprocessor chips, sur-rounded them with all the other stuff you need to interact with a computer, and we made a computer that was about thirteen pounds. And people would look at it and say, 'Well, where's the computer? This is just the terminal,' and we'd say, 'No, that is the computer.' And after about five minutes of repeating this, finally a light bulb would go on in their minds, and they'd decide if they didn't like it and they could throw it out the window or run over it with their car. But this was the entire computer. That's why we exist: fractional-horsepower com-puting. It's created a revolution. It was invented in 1976, the first personal computer. This year, in 1983, the industry's going to ship over three million of the little buggers. Three million! By 1986 we're going to ship more computers than automobiles in this country.

Let me digress for a minute. One of the reasons I'm here is because I need your help. If you've looked at computers, they look like garbage. All the great product designers are off designing automobiles or buildings. But hardly any of them are designing computers. If we take a look, we're going to sell three million computers this year, ten million in '86, whether they look like a piece of shit or they look great. People are just going to suck this stuff up so fast no matter what it looks like. And it doesn't cost any more money to make them look great. They're going to be these new objects that are going to be in everyone's working envi-ronment, everyone's educational environment and everyone's home environment. We have a shot of putting a great object there; and if we don't, we're going to put one more piece-of-junk object there. By '86, '87, pick a year, people are going to spend more time interacting with these machines than

they do interacting with automobiles today. People are going to be spending two, three hours a day, interacting with these machines – longer than they spend in the car.

And so, the industrial design, the software design and how people interact with these things certainly must be given the consideration that we give automobiles today, if not a lot more. And what we've got is a situation where most automobiles are not being designed in the United States. Televisions? Audio-electronics? Watches, cameras, bicycles, calculators, you name it – most of the objects of our lives are not designed in America. We've blown it. We've blown it from an industrial point of view because we've lost the markets to foreign competitors. We've also blown it from a design point of view. And I think we have a chance with this new computing technology meeting people in the eighties – the fact that computers and society are out on a first date in the eighties. We have a chance to make these things beautiful, and we have a chance to communicate something through the design of the objects themselves.

In addition to that, we're going to spend over a hundred million dollars in the next twelve months on media advertising for Apple alone. IBM will spend at least an equivalent amount. We generate tens of millions of dollars' worth of brochures, posters – more than the auto industry, again, as a comparison. And this stuff can either be great, or it can be lousy. And we need help — we really, really need your help.

OK, let's go back to this revolution. What's happening is that the personal computer is a new medium of communication – one of *the* media. So what's a medium? A book is a medium. Telephone, radio, television – these are mediums of commu-nication. And each medium has shortcomings, boundaries you can't cross, but it also generally has some new, unique opportunities. The neat thing is that each medium shapes not only the communication that goes through it, but it shapes the process of communication. Perfect example: if you compare the telephone to what we're seeing now in electronic mail, we see that indeed, in one sense we're sending a voice through these wires and in another sense we're sending ones and zeros. So the content that's travelling through these mediums is certainly different. The most interesting thing that's different is the process of communi-cation. If I talk on the telephone with anyone, we both must be on the phone at the same time. But when I'm working, when I want to send something to somebody with a computer terminal, they don't need to be there. They can retrieve it at 12am. They can retrieve it three days later. They can be in New York and retrieve it. One of these days when we've

People are going to be spending two, three hours a day interacting with these machines – longer than they spend in the car.

got portable computers with radio links, they can be walking around Aspen and retrieve it. And so the process of communication itself changes as the mediums evolve.

What I'm claiming is that computers are a medium. Personal computers are a new and different medium from large computers. What happens when a new medium enters the scene is we tend to fall back into old media habits. Let's look at a few transitions from one medium to another, radio to television, television to this incredible new interactive medium of the video disk. If you go back and look at the first television shows, they're basically radio shows with a television camera pointed at them. And it took us the better part of the fifties to really understand how television was going to come into its own. I really think that the first time that a lot of people were shook into realizing that television had come of age was the JFK funeral. The nation, a lot of the world, experienced the JFK funeral in their living room at a level of intensity that wouldn't have been possible with radio. Another more upbeat example was the Apollo landing. That experience was not possible with the previous medium, and yet it took us the best part of twenty years for that one to really evolve.

Let's look at the next transition: we have this optical video disk which can store 55,000

images on a side, or an hour of video, randomly accessible. What are we using it for? Movies. We're dropping back into the old media habits. There are a few experiments, though, that are starting to happen, and we're starting to believe that five years, ten years from now it's going to come into its own. MIT came out about four years ago, and they had this truck with this camera on it, and photographed every single intersection in every single street in Aspen. They photographed all the buildings. And they got this computer and this video disk hooked up together, and on the screen you see yourself looking down a street, and there you can touch the screen, there are some arrows on the screen, and you can touch 'Walk Forward' and it's just like you're walking forward in the street. You get to an intersection and you can stop. You can look right, and you can look straight, and you can look left, and you can decide which way you want to go. You can even look in some of the shops. It's an electronic map that gives you the feeling that you're walking through Aspen. Then there's four little buttons in the corner, because they came back and they did the same thing for all four seasons. So you're looking down a street – hit 'Winter' – all of a sudden you're looking down the same street with three feet of snow on it. It's really amazing. That's not incredibly useful, but it points to some of the interactive nature of this medium that's just starting to break out from movies, and it's going to take another five or ten years to evolve.

OK, let's go back to computers. We're in the 'I Love Lucy' stage right now, in our medium development. What we did was microcomputers, personal computers, first coming on the scene. What do we do? We fall back into old, media habits, the kind of stuff we have been doing on them historically. And we're just starting to break out of it now. I'm not an artist in the sense that many of you are, but I can sit down and draw artistic pictures with this program called Lisa Draw. If I don't like what I've just drawn I can erase it, I can move it, I can shrink it, I can change its texture. There's a little airbrush. The more I scrub the darker it gets. I can put soft edges on things, hard edges on things. And so, with no talent at drawing at all, I can make neat drawings. I can then cut them out and paste them into my documents, so that I can combine pictures and words. And then I can send it on the electronic mailbox to somebody else, living here in Aspen; I can dial up their phone number and get their mail, they can see this drawing that I made. So we're starting to break out, and you can just see it now, and it's really exciting.

So where we are is that the personal computer is a new medium, and that it's now in the eighties that society and computers are really meeting for the first time. In fifteen years it's going to be all over in terms of this first phase, getting these tools out into society in large numbers. But during these next fifteen years, we have an opportunity to do it great, or do it so-so, and what a lot of us at Apple are working on is trying to do it great.

We're going to look at one last thing. What is a computer program? Do you know what a computer program is? Anybody? No? Sort of? It's an odd thing. It's really an odd thing. You've never seen an electron, but computer programs have no physical manifestation at all. They're simply ideas expressed on paper. Computer programs are archetypal – what do I mean by that? Let's compare computer programming to television programming. Again, if you go back and you look at the tapes of JFK's funeral in 1963, you'll start to cry. You will feel a lot of the same feelings you felt when watching that twenty years ago. Why? Because through the art of television programming, we are very good at capturing a set of experiences. You can really feel the excitement of Neil Armstrong landing on the moon. Computer programming does something a little bit different. What computer programming does is capture the underlying principles of an experience, not the experience itself, but the underlying principles of the experience. Those principles can

enable thousands of different experiences that all follow those laws, if you will. The perfect example is the video game. What does a video game do? It follows the laws of gravity, of angular momentum, and it sets up this stupid little pong game. The ball always follows these laws. No two pong games are ever the same. And yet every single pong game follows these underlying principles ... It's an interactive way of learning that none of us ever had growing up. The game can produce thousands of individual experiences, but all based on that one set of underlying principles.

When I was going to school, I had a few great teachers and a lot of mediocre teachers. And the thing that probably kept me out of jail was the books. I could go and read what Aristotle or Plato wrote, without an intermediary in the way. And a book was a phenomenal thing. It got right from the source to the destination, without anything in the middle. The problem was, you can't ask Aristotle a question. And I think as we look towards the next fifty to a hundred years, if we really can come up with these machines that can capture an underlying spirit, or an underlying set of principles, or an underlying way of looking at the world, then when the next Aristotle comes around, maybe if he carries around one of these machines with him his whole life – his or her whole life – and types in all this stuff, then maybe someday after this person's dead and gone, we can ask this machine, 'Hey, what would Aristotle have said? What about this?' And maybe we won't get the right answer, but maybe we will. And that's really exciting to me. And that's one of the reasons I'm doing what I'm doing.

So what do you want to talk about?

BIOGRAPHIES

Author Biographies

Jennifer Dunlop Fletcher is the Helen Hilton Raiser Curator of Architecture and Design at the San Francisco Museum of Modern Art. Since 2008 she has contributed to the museum's Architecture and Design programme through acquisitions and exhibitions, with a focus on visionary designers and movements of the past forty years. Recent curatorial projects include *Bureau Spectacular: insideoutsidebetweenbeyond* (2017), *Typeface to Interface* (2016), *Lebbeus Woods, Architect* (2013), *A Quincy Jones: Building for Better Living* (2013) and *The Utopian Impulse: Buckminster Fuller and the Bay Area* (2012). Jennifer is a graduate of New York University, and earned master's degrees from Bard College in curatorial studies and Harvard University in architecture history and theory.

Jonathan Ive is Apple's chief design officer. He is responsible for all design at Apple, including the look and feel of Apple hardware, user interface, packaging, major architectural projects such as Apple Campus 2 and Apple's retail stores, as well as new ideas and future initiatives. Since 1996 Jony has led Apple's design team. He holds over 5,000 patents and has been recognized with numerous design awards, including the Design Museum London's first Designer of the Year in 2003, the Design and Art Direction (D&AD) President's Award in 2005 and the Cooper Hewitt, Smithsonian Design Museum's Product Design Award in 2007. A native of London, Jony was made a Knight Commander of the British Empire in 2013 for 'services to design and enterprise'.

Barry M Katz is consulting professor in the Department of Mechanical Engineering at Stanford University, professor of Industrial and Interaction Design at the California College of the Arts in San Francisco, and fellow at IDEO, the Silicon Valley-based design and innovation consultancy. He is the author of six books, including *Make It New: The History of Silicon Valley Design* (2015), *NONOBJECT* with Branko Lukic (2011) and *Change by Design* with Tim Brown (2009). His writings on design as a strategy of innovation have appeared in many academic, professional and popular journals.

Peter Lunenfeld is a professor and vice chair of UCLA's Design Media Arts department and is on the faculties of the Digital Humanities and Urban Humanities programmes. His work can be mapped via a lumpy Venn diagram that includes media philosophy, design theory, art criticism, urban history and digital humanities. Recent publications include *Digital_Humanities* (2012), co-authored with Anne Burdick, Johanna Drucker, Todd Presner and Jeffrey Schnapp, *The Secret War Between Downloading and Uploading* (2011), winner of the 2013 Lee Prize for Scholarship, and *USER: InfoTechnoDemo* (2005). He received an International Award for Art Criticism (IAAC) in 2016, and is working on an alternate, connectionist history of Southern California.

Brendan McGetrick is an independent writer, curator and designer. His work has appeared in publications in over thirty countries, including *the New York Times*, *Wired*, the *Financial Times*, *Art Review*, *Der Spiegel*, *Domus* and *Vogue Nippon*. He is the editor and author of six books, including *Urban China: Work in Progress* (2011), *MAD Dinner* (2010) and *Content* (2004). In 2014 he co-curated the Russian Pavilion at the Venice Biennale, together with Anton Kalgaev and Dasha Paramonova. Since 2015 he has served as director and curator of Global Grad Show, an international exhibition of graduate design.

Justin McGuirk is a writer and curator based in London. He is chief curator at the Design Museum and the head of Design Curating and Writing at Design Academy Eindhoven. He has been the director of Strelka Press, the design critic of the *Guardian* and the editor of *Icon* magazine. In 2012 he was awarded the Golden Lion at the Venice Biennale of Architecture for an exhibition he curated with Urban Think Tank. His book *Radical Cities: Across Latin America in Search of a New Architecture* was published in 2014.

Simon Sadler teaches the history and theory of architecture and design at the University of California, Davis, where he is a professor in the Department of Design. His publications include *Archigram: Architecture without Architecture* (2005), *Non-Plan: Essays on Freedom, Participation and Change in Modern Architecture and Urbanism* (2000), co-edited with Jonathan Hughes, *The Situationist City* (1998) and numerous essays and articles on counterculture and design in California. His commentary on Californian design has been featured in *Boom: A Journal of California*, the online journal *Places* and the *New York Times*.

Louise Sandhaus is a graphic designer and graphic design educator. She was previously director of the Graphic Design programme at California Institute of the Arts (CalArts) where she is currently a faculty member. She is the author of *Earthquakes, Mudslides, Fires and Riots: California and Graphic Design 1936–1986* (2014). The publication received the Palme D'Argent for best art book at the International Festival of Art Books and Films on Art (FILAF) in 2015, among many other global recognitions.

Deyan Sudjic is director of the Design Museum in London. His career has spanned journalism, teaching and writing. Previously he was director of the Glasgow UK City of Architecture and Design programme in 1999 and director of the Venice Architecture Biennale in 2002. He was editor of *Domus* magazine from 2000 to 2004, and founding editor of *Blueprint* magazine from 1983 to 1996. His portfolio of publications includes *Ettore Sottsass and the Poetry of Things* (2015), *B is for Bauhaus* (2014), *Norman Foster: A Life in Architecture* (2010), *The Language of Things* (2008) and *The Edifice Complex* (2006). He was made an OBE in 2000.

Interviewee Biographies

Yves Béhar is a designer fusing new technologies, entrepreneurial innovation and human experiences. He is the founder and chief designer of fuseproject, a design, digital experience and branding firm that he established in 1999.

Matías Duarte leads the Material Design team at Google, and is responsible for design consistency, design tools and User Experience (UX) best practices. Prior to founding Material Design, Matías was vice president of Design for Android.

April Greiman is a designer and artist exploring image, word and colour as objects in time and space. Instrumental in the use and acceptance of advanced technology in the creative process, she is widely recognized for her revolutionary digital imaging work.

David Kelley is the founder and chairman of the global design and innovation company, IDEO. He also founded Stanford University's Hasso Plattner Institute of Design, known as the d.school.

Kevin Kelly is senior maverick at *Wired* magazine. He co-founded *Wired* in 1993, and served as its executive editor for its first seven years. He was also publisher and editor of the *Whole Earth Review*, a journal of unorthodox technical news.

Fred Turner is the Harry and Norman Chandler Professor and chair of the Department of Communication at Stanford University. Before coming to Stanford, he taught at Harvard and MIT. He also worked for ten years as a journalist.

INDEX

INDEX

INDEX

PICTURE CREDITS

PICTURE CREDITS

Every reasonable effort has been made to acknowledge the ownership of copyright for photographs included in this volume. Any errors that may have occurred are inadvertent, and will be corrected in subsequent editions provided notification is sent in writing to the publisher.

ACKNOWLEDGEMENTS

This book was published in conjunction with the exhibition *California: Designing Freedom* at the Design Museum, London, 24 May–15 October 2017.

Curators: Justin McGuirk and Brendan McGetrick
Curatorial Assistant: Kyle Osbrink
Project Manager: Silvia Bordin
Exhibitions Coordinator: Cleo Stringer
Senior Technician: Stuart Robertson
Curatorial Research Assistant: Alex Todd

Exhibition Design: Plaid
Exhibition Graphic Design: Barnbrook

The editors and curators would like to thank the following organizations and people for their enthusiastic support:
Apple / Jonathan Ive
Google / Corinne Onetto, Rob Giampietro and
        Gaja Sidrys Caple
Waymo / Meiling Tan, Yoojung Ahn
SFMoMA / Jennifer Dunlop Fletcher
Computer History Museum / Dag Spicer
Corita Art Center / Keri Marken
ONE Archives / David Evans Frantz
Skatelab / Todd Huber
Herman Miller
Facebook / Christiana Chae, Kara Fong,
        Shali Nguyen
Facebook Analog Research Laboratory /
        Scott Boms
Make Magazine
ACLU / Marcus F Benigno
Oakland Museum of California / Brittany Bradley
Free Speech Movement Archives / Barbara Stack
USC Institute for Creative Technologies /
        Albert "Skip" Rizzo
Stanford d.school / Scott Doorley, Scott Witthoft
Autodesk / Rama Dunayevich, Cornelia Scheitz
The Amplifier Foundation / Cleo Barnett
GOOD / Kritika Misra
BAMPFA / Lisa Calden
Burning Man Project / Joe Meschede
IDEO

We would also like to thank the following individuals for their invaluable advice and generosity:
Ian Lynch Smith and Colin Lynch Smith
Fred Turner
Barry M Katz
Kevin Kelly
Lloyd Kahn
Rudy VanderLans
Neil Feineman
Syd Mead
Mark McCloud
John Plunkett
Erik Adigard
Sheila Levrant de Bretteville
Emory Douglas
Paul Prejza
Glen Keane
Dusty Reid
Jeff Decker
Bernhard Drax
Valerie Casey
Arnold Wasserman
David Greenberg
April Greiman
Alex McDowell

Phaidon Press Limited
Regent's Wharf
All Saints Street
London N1 9PA

Phaidon Press Inc.
65 Bleecker Street
New York, NY 10012

phaidon.com

In partnership with
the Design Museum
224–238 Kensington High Street
London W8 6AG

designmuseum.org

First Published in 2017
© 2017 Phaidon Press Limited
Texts © 2017 the Design Museum

ISBN 978 0 7148 7423 4

A CIP catalogue record for this book is available from the British Library
and the Library of Congress.

Phaidon Press Limited
Commissioning Editor: Virginia McLeod
Project Editor: Robyn Taylor
Production Controller: Adela Cory
Designers: Jonathan Abbott, Jonathan Barnbrook,
Jelena Lugonja and Simona Materazzini at Barnbrook

the Design Museum
Publishing Manager: Mark Cortes Favis
Publishing Coordinator: Ianthe Fry
Picture Researcher: Anabel Navarro Llorens
Editorial Assistants: Caroline Hanna, Kyle Osbrink and Alex Todd

Printed in Italy